JOHANN SEBASTIAN

JOHANN SEBASTIAN

A Tercentenary Celebration

EDITED BY
SEYMOUR L. BENSTOCK

Prepared under the auspices of Hofstra University

Contributions to the Study of Music and Dance, Number 19

GREENWOOD PRESS
Westport, Connecticut • London

Library of Congress Cataloging-in-Publication Data

Johann Sebastian : a tercentenary celebration / edited by Seymour L.
  Benstock ; prepared under the auspices of Hofstra University.
      p.   cm.—(Contributions to the study of music and dance,
  ISSN 0193-9041 ; no. 19)
    Includes bibliographical references.
    Contents: The contemporizing of scripture in the cantatas of
  Johann Sebastian Bach / Howard C. Adams—J.S. Bach : the flauto
  and the traverso / Samuel Baron—An odd couple : J.S. Bach and
  A.S. Huxley / Ann Edward Bennis—Hemiola in the eighteenth century /
  Vincent Corrigan—The "unravelling" of Schoenberg's Bach / John J.
  Daverio—The message of Johann Sebastian Bach in Ingmar Bergman's
  cinematic art / Fritz Sammern-Frankenegg—Bach's Musical offering
  as autobiography / Stephen A. Gottlieb—Bach and Edwards on the
  religious affections / Richard A. Spurgeon Hall—Bach the
  architect : some remarks on structure and pacing in selected
  Praeludia / Charles M. Joseph—Musical expression and musical
  rhetoric in the keyboard works of J.S. Bach / David Schulenberg—
  The original circumstances in the performance of Bach's Leipzig
  church cantatas, Wegen seiner Sonn- und Festtägigen Amts-
  Verrichtungen / Don L. Smithers.
    ISBN 0-313-27441-X (lib. bdg. : alk. paper)
    1. Bach, Johann Sebastian, 1685-1750—Criticism and
  interpretation. I. Benstock, Seymour L. II. Hofstra University.
  III. Series.
  ML410.B1J63   1992
  780'.92—dc20   90-32455

British Library Cataloguing in Publication Data is available.

Library of Congress Catalog Card Number: 90-32455
ISBN: 0-313-27441-X
ISSN: 0193-9041

First published in 1992

Greenwood Press, 88 Post Road West, Westport, CT 06881
An imprint of Greenwood Publishing Group, Inc.

Printed in the United States of America

The paper used in this book complies with the
Permanent Paper Standard issued by the National
Information Standards Organization (Z39.48-1984).

10 9 8 7 6 5 4 3 2 1

FOR

C.M.B.

Contents

Preface

The genius of Johann Sebastian Bach transcends time, national boundaries, and disciplines. The collection of essays in this volume reveals a composer who has influenced not only his fellow composers and performers but has touched literature, film, religion, and psychology. His message is an enduring one. Explanations of his genius are only first steps toward understanding the humanity of this great figure.

I wish to thank the members of the Hofstra Cultural Center for their help in assembling this collection; without their dedication, this journal would not have come to fruition. The format of the various articles, while holding to some degree of uniformity, also allows for the desires of the individual contributors. My personal thanks to the authors for their patience, and to Judith D'Angio for her patience and understanding in the final preparation of the manuscript of this volume.

JOHANN SEBASTIAN

1

The Contemporizing of Scripture in the Cantatas of Johann Sebastian Bach

Howard C. Adams

There is much to be said and much that has been said about the use of
Scripture in Bach's cantatas. Scholars have noted the constriction on
the church composer by the strict use of the lectionary and have been
amazed at the variety in Bach's creative use of assigned texts. Sometimes the texts are treated exegetically, with comments designed to throw
light on the message. Sometimes the treatment of the text is almost
homiletic, with the hearers exhorted to go forth into the world with a
new sense of Christian commitment to a task. In other cantatas one passage of Scripture is pitted against another for the light and harmony
that are emitted from them—an extension of the Lutheran practice of interpreting Scripture by Scripture. However, what is probably the most
exciting element in the treatment of Scripture in the cantatas has been
little noted: the continual and urgent move toward contemporizing biblical texts--toward treating ancient texts as if they were contemporary
documents about contemporary life. I am not, of course, claiming this is
new; anyone who has added a vocal and intellectual decibel to Johan
Heermann's Herzliebster Jesu set by Johann Cruger knows it is not.
Neither am I claiming a monolithic unity to the texts of the cantatas,
which were written by many hands. However, they do have a unity to them
in that they come from the Lutheran Pietistic tradition, and in that they
were all chosen by the composer. It seems evident that many of the texts
were selected for their emphasis on contemporaneity, since, as Bach's
music interprets the words, this quality is both marked and moving.
    The Cantatas contain a raft of short references that tie Scriptural
passages to the contemporary congregations at worship. Cantata 64 answers the Scriptural proclamation, "Behold what manner of Love the father
hath bestowed," with a Martin Luther chorale, "He has done all this to
show his great love for us; may all Christendom rejoice over it." Cantata
4 looks backward to connect Easter with a Paschal Lamb of the Old Testament, and then identifies the lamb's blood with that of Christ "burned"
on the cross in "hot love," and further brings the event into Bach's own
century by affirming, "This blood identifies our door." When the bass
cites the book of Revelation in Cantata 61, "Behold I stand at the door
and knock," the soprano responds pointedly, "stand open, my heart: Jesus
comes and enters in." The same Scripture receives short comment in the
second person in Cantata 180 when the tenor urges: "Wake up: your savior
is knocking. Open up your heart's door right away." The aria continues
in rollicking melody exhorting the congregation to respond in "gebrochne
Freidenworte"--"broken joywords." In Cantata 105, the choir's rendition
of the 141st Psalm," Enter not into judgment with Thy servant, O Lord,"
is immediately personalized and contemporized by the alto, who responds
with the plea, "Don't cast me away, my God, while I am bowing in humility

before you, before your face," which then modulates into a personal confession.   Timothy's first-century biblical injunction to remember that Christ was raised from the dead is reiterated by the choir in Cantata 67 and immediately evokes a response from an eighteenth-century tenor who ask why, in spite of his faith in the resurrection, he is still afraid; in his anxiety he calls for a new appearance of his savior. The biblical identification of Christ with the morning star in Cantata 96 is followed by a cry from the tenor that the star's light might illuminate his soul "that it might recognize you by faith, that it might burn with holy flames. Oh, work up in me a believer's thirst after you." The soprano recitative which follows shows no less a personal, first-person longing for the light of the star which continues to shine in the eighteenth century: "Lead me, O God, unenlightened as I am, into the right way, for my flesh is so often inclined to err." Finally the bass follows suit. Confessing that he tends to wander erroneously first to the right and then to the left, he pleads with Christ to lead him now to heaven's gate. In Cantata 52, the threatening falseness of the world is movingly described and then summed up in a biblical event which typifies the morality of Bach's current world: "When Joab kisses, then must some upright Abner die." In the rest of the cantata, the soprano affirms that she has a continuing source of truth and personal protection that makes the evil of her contemporary world irrelevant: "God, who intends to deal honestly with me, remains my friend."

One of the most obvious occasions for the contemporization of Scripture comes at Christmas, and the German tradition of placing a crib in the church probably added to the sensitivity of Bach's librettists. Thus, after Cantata 62 sings its praise to the wonder and glory of the Incarnation, in the closing duet Bach's soprano and alto approach the crib itself: "We express honor for this glory and come now to your crib, praising with joyful lips what you have prepared for us. The darkness no longer frightens us now that we see your unending light." Cantata 65 celebrates the event on a much wider scale. The chorus begins with a text from the sixtieth chapter of Isaiah: "From Sheba will they all arrive bringing gold and incense." The bass moves the time one step forward to its fulfillment at the birth of Jesus, and then completes the move into his own time: "I also must turn to your manger and likewise must be thankful, for today is my day of joy". The gift he offers, however, is not frankincense but his heart, and in an aria he invites others to join him by presenting their own. The heart, adds the tenor recitative, is no less a gift than those of the wise men, for it contains "the gold of faith, the incense of prayer, and the myrrh of patience," his very personal gifts. The text of Cantata 121 is more ponderous in its theologizing of the Incarnation, and the bass aria, noting that John's joyous leap in the womb was a recognition of Christ, adds that the singer's heart ought also to "force its way eagerly from the world to your crib." The soprano then comments on the emotional enormity of the Incarnation and contemporizes it by herself joining the choir of angels assembled at Christ's birth: "Yet how can I look at you in your crib? My heart sighs with lips trembling and nearly closed; it brings its thank-offering to this place. God who was boundless in size takes on poverty and the form of a servant, and because he has done this for our good, so I, along with the angel choirs, will sound forth a triumphant song of praise and thanks." There is no apparent incongruity in having an eighteenth-century soprano singing exultantly in a first-century choir. Thanksgiving and joy also mark Cantata 63's response to the Incarnation. The invitation, "Come and hurry to the crib with me," comes from the opening chorus, and later an alto-tenor duet adds resonance to the joy: "Come, Christians, come to the round-dance. You shall rejoice in what God has done this day."

Cantata 18, which develops a theme of fertility, represents a more

extended use of contemporization.   It opens with a sinfonia, after which
the bass, in recitative, introduces the Old Testament text: "Even as the
rain and snow fall from heaven and do not return but fertilize the earth
..., so shall it be with my word."   In appropriating this text to his own
time, the tenor also responds to the Gospel for the day, the parable of
the sower, as he offers his heart as fertile soil for the Word-seed: "My
God, here will my heart be: I open it up to you in my Jesus's name.
Strew your seed as you would into good soil.   Let my heart bring forth
fruit a hundred-fold." The bass hints at the parable of the tares when he
asks help against the devil, who would rob him of the Word, and the tenor
echoes many New Testament exhortations to bear fruit when he warns that
many "disown both faith and the word and fall like rotten fruit," an action illustrated by Bach's dramatically descending run on the word "fall."
    Cantata 108, written for Pentecost, opens with an arioso proclama-
tion of Scripture from the bass: "It is expedient for you that I go away,
for if I go not away, the Comforter will not come unto you; but if I
depart, I will send him unto you."   The tenor answers with an aria of
faith addressed directly across the years to Christ, but responds more
personally to the Scripture passage in an ensuing recitative paradoxically combining an affirmation with a question: "Your Spirit will so rule me
that I will walk on the right path.   By your leaving he will come to me.
Anxiously I ask, Oh, isn't he here already?"   The question mixes historical eras; it is addresseed to a Christ still on earth, while also being
spoken, or sung, in a worshipping congregation at Pentecost which is
celebrating the presence of the spirit that has followed the departure of
Christ from the earth.
    Cantata 148 is entirely a contemporaneous response to Scripture. The
opening chorus proclaims the twenty-ninth Psalm ("Worship the Lord in the
beauty of holiness") and the tenor responds, "I rush to hear the teach-
ings of life."   If Bach in the rest of the aria was responding to his own
setting of the psalm, it would indeed be justified: "How beautifully do
the blessed cry out their joyful noise in praise of the Highest!"   The
alto recitative introduces a new psalm (number forty-two) proclaiming:
"Just as the stag cries for fresh water, so I cry to you, O God," and
puts the psalm into the context of current worship.   In the aria that
follows, the panting of the heart for water and the worshipper for the
Word is reiterated in gorgeous melody, making the love-longing for God a
poignantly personal hunger for the Eucharist that almost borders on the
sexual: "My mouth and my heart stand open to you, most high; sink yourself therein ["senke dich hinein"--to a descending cadence]:   I in you
and you in me. Faith, love, patient endurance, and hope shall be my bed
of quietness."
    Although the overtones of sexual love in Christianity often sound
strange to twentieth-century ears, worshippers in the eighteenth century
were much more accustomed to intimacy in the love between Jesus and the
soul.   It was common to apply the love songs of the Song of Solomon as
allegorically representing, or typologically "shadowing forth" the love
of Christ for his Church, and, according to the piety of the time, for
each member of the Church. The love duets between the soul and Jesus in
Cantata 140 (Wachet Auf) are well known and fit the biblical context of
the parable of the wise virgins waiting for Christ the bridegroom at the
wedding feast.   Cantata 32, which begins "Dearest Jesus, object of my
longing," seems to combine the longing of Mary to find Jesus when he was
left behind in the temple at the age of twelve with the longing of the
Shunamite maiden for her absent love in the Song of Solomon.   In recitative, the soul, a soprano, fairly exults when she finds her love: "My
body and soul are happy in the living God. Ah, Jesus, my heart now loves
you eternally."   To this outburst Jesus answers, "You can be this happy
when heart and spirit are aflame with love for me." This love is finally
fulfilled in a duet when both lovers, Jesus and the soul, unite mystical-

ly to sing: "Now I will never leave you, and furthermore I will continually hug you." The drama of longing and fulfillment is even more poignant, if possible, in Cantata 49. Here Jesus as the bridegroom "searches with longing" and prepares the wedding feast for his bride. The soul hears and answers, "I fall at your feet"; together Jesus and the soul sing, "Come, o most beautiful, come and let yourself be kissed," and together they "enjoy the rich feast." Interestingly, the soul in her wedding garments is not in an attitude of humility, confessing sin, but rather stands up, proud to sing joyously, "I am glorious, I am beautiful, in order to enflame my savior." Although this reflects a mutuality that makes love possible, it is still the soul's faith that allows her to don the finery of the wedding garments, which themselves consist of "the justification of his redemption." This mystic wedding of Christ and the soul is, of course, a special instance of the contemporization of the Scripture, or of the Christ of Scripture, and may require a paper of its own to do justice to Bach's musical treatment of it.

The most outwardly dramatic contemporization in the cantatas takes place in those works in which the singers virtually enter into the world of the biblical narrative. In Cantata 159, for example, the biblical scene is Caesarea Philippi, where Jesus announces his intention to go to Jerusalem. The tenor comments on the difficulty of the road, made worse by his own sins, and finally calls out dramatically across the chasm of time to his Lord, "Don't go! The cross is already erected on which you shall bleed to death. One is seeking whips and another is binding rods. Don't go there!" An instant's reflection, however, reminds him of the consequences should Jesus take his advice and refuse to travel to Jerusalem and the cross. It would mean a much more difficult path for himself—even the road to Hell.

The alto soloist then takes up the situation, and as so often in the cantatas (and the Passions) responds with a tender love which obliterates time. The road to the cross cannot be avoided, but the singer (like Peter) vows to follow "through spittle and shame" to embrace Jesus on the cross, to keep Him in her (or his) heart, and finally, to become His grave. The bass aria that follows theologizes on the new-bought freedom from sin and, still in the contemporary mode, adds, "I will now rush to my Jesus and bestow thanks." Even the closing chorale maintains the present tense in addressing Christ and confirming the ultimate paradox of the cross: "Jesus, your passion is sheer joy to me; your wounds, crown, and shame are pasture for my heart. If I think about it, my soul walks on roses. Prepare a dwelling place for me in heaven."

There is an element of whimsey in Cantata 175, which opens with a short biblical recitative in which the tenor sings, "He calls his own sheep by name and leads them out." The alto immediately contemporizes this in a plaintive aria, adopting the role of a hungry lamb: "Come, lead me, my shepherd, my joy. My spirit longs for green pasture; my heart languishes, it groans day and night." The tenor recitative that follows identifies the sinner as a contemporary lost lamb longing to be found, and the succeeding aria responds to the biblical passage theologically: The true shepherd is recognized by the door through which he enters, and the lamb adopts him by faith.

Cantata 81 does not begin with a passage of Scripture, but the lectionary passage for the day was presumably fresh in the congregation's mind, since the cantatas were sung immediately after the reading of the Gospel. It is certainly clear from the complaint of the opening alto aria that she (or he, in Bach's day) has joined the disciples in their small boat on the Sea of Galilee: "Jesus is asleep, what hope can I have? Don't I, with ashen face, see the abyss of death wide open before me?" The tenor recitative that follows likewise addresses Christ as a contemporary, describing the sleep of Jesus in terms of distance, and, even more interestingly, in terms of the light hidden by the closed eyelids,

never before shut in a time of need. "You indeed directed the newly-
converted wise men along the right way to travel by providing a star.
Now lead me by the light from your eyes, for there is nothing but danger
ahead on this road [Weg]." In the ensuing aria, the tenor connects the
storm at sea (in the midst of which Jesus is asleep) with the threatening
waves of the ungodly which continually try to weaken him, even though as
a Christian he is expected (somewhat unjustly, he would seem to imply) to
stand firm against such forces. At this point the bass, at exactly the
right moment, interposes the direct Scripture on which turns the whole
structure of the cantata: "O Ye of little faith, why are ye so fearful?"
(Matt. 8:26). His aria elaborates on Christ's succinct "Be still" by
augmenting the address to the storm: "Quiet down, storm and wind! May
your boundaries be so limited that the accident can over harm my chosen
child." The alto, who made the opening complaint, appropriately responds
in recitative: "It is good for me that Jesus speaks a word. My helper
being awake, the storm of the waves, the misfortune of the night, and all
trouble must disappear." The cantata ends appropriately with a chorale
set to the words of Johann Franck, again setting Christ's "Peace, be
still" in a contemporary mode: "Under your shelter I am free from the
storms of all enemies. Though Satan may have my scent and the enemy be
aroused, Jesus will always stand by me. In spite of my fears of sin and
hell, he will protect me from current thunder and lightning."

Many of the same dramatic elements are found in Cantata 11, written
to celebrate the Ascension. After a chorus of praise, the tenor recites
the Scripture, which is in the past tense: "And it came to pass, while
He blessed them, He was parted from them." The bass recitative that follows addresses Jesus as a contemporary. The singers respond as if they,
in the eighteenth century, were in the presence of Christ in one of the
fields of Palestine: "Ah, Jesus, is it already the hour for you to depart, when we must let you go? See how hot tears are rolling down our
pale cheeks." Again it is the alto who receives the tenderest melody
(later used for the "Agnus Dei" in the Mass in B Minor) and the more personal lyrics: "Ah, stay with me, my dearest life, don't go so soon. Your
farewell and early departure bring me the greatest of all sorrow. Stay,
or I will be completely surrounded with pain [Schmerz]." The tenor and
bass return to Scripture, and in the words of the two men in white cloth-
ing, admonish the first-and eighteenth-century watchers: "Ye men of Galilee, why stand ye gazing up into heaven? This same Jesus, which is taken
up from you into heaven, shall so come in like manner as ye have seen him
go into heaven." Again it is the eighteenth-century alto who takes up
the response, addressing the first-century Christ: "Oh, come back soon;
. . . otherwise every moment will be hateful to me and will seem to last
for years." The tenor reiterates Scripture, repeating the passage that
describes the return to Jerusalem with worship and joy. The soprano
speaks from an eternal more than a contemporary context, affirming that
though the body is ascended, the love remains and binds past, present,
and future: "Your love remains with me so that I can be revived in the
Spirit here and now, in this time, by the future glory, when we will
stand before you." The closing chorus looks only to the future "when we
shall kiss the saviour."

Bach's cantatas are indeed dramatic in form. Recently, a radio
commentator on the Public Broadcasting System called Bach's cantatas
"Operas in miniature." Although this is surely an overstatement, the
cantatas are indeed rich in drama, much of which is achieved by the dramatic movement of contemporary singers directly into biblical situations,
giving a sense of reality and urgency to a genuine experience of the
cantatas.

2

J. S. Bach: The Flauto and the Traverso

Samuel Baron

Tone color, range, technical capability, expressive profile--these are the elements that add up to what we might call the personality of a musical instrument. Composers employ these personalities in their work, calling on the various instruments to play roles in the scenarios that are their compositions.

J. S. Bach, especially in his Leipzig period, stood ready to create what was for him a new language, a language in which all the musical elements--melody, rhythm, harmony, and tone colors (instrumentation), would subordinate themselves to the setting of texts. These texts, and the religious emotions of which they are the manifestation and in whose world they have their only true existence, would set the limits of the composer's efforts. Their musical expression would become the true judge of the composer's work.

In this paper I will discuss the use Bach made of two similar instruments that were part of his world of sound, two instruments that were closely related in his lifetime yet were destined to describe contrasting trajectories in their future life stories. These instruments were known to Bach as the flauto and the traverso (or traversiere, to give it the French appellation which Bach often used in tribute to its French origin). To us they are known as the recorder, which is essentially unchanged since Bach's time, and the flute, an evolved mutant of the instrument that Bach first heard (most likely) in Dresden in 1718, where it was played by the mighty Pierre-Gabriel Buffardin.

The recorder was on a downward curve of popularity, and the flute on an upward curve. The flauto became so out of fashion (imagine a recorder in a Beethoven symphony) that it was ignored by composers and was thus able to stay unchanged, unevolved, and unimproved for centuries. The traverso stayed at the forefront of modern developments and evolved from a keyless form through three, four, five, and more key versions, and finally to a generously mechanized form in Theobald Boehm's ingenious version of 1847. It also changed its bore from conical to cylindrical, and went from wood to metal. It became a fixture of symphonic orchestral music. However, this was not on Bach's mind at all, and could not have been known to him. To Bach, the flauto was an old friend, and the traverso a promising newcomer; he saw both of them as potentially useful to him in his new position.

The Flauto in Bach Cantatas

If we examine the use of the recorder in the Bach cantata music, we come to see that Bach assigned it a special affective role. By linking the use of the instrument to the texts with which it is associated (especially in the arias), it becomes clear that Bach found its musical personality fitted to the expression of moods and emotions related to sad and mournful states. The characteristic nuance of the recorder is the sigh; its very sound droops. In the opening movement of <u>Cantata 13</u>, an aria for tenor with <u>oboe da caccia obbligato</u>, two recorders, and <u>continuo</u> we find the text:

> <u>Meine Seufzer, meine Thränen</u>   My sighs, my tears
> <u>können nicht zu zählen sein.</u>   cannot be counted.

The two recorders provide the framework for this piece.

> 182/5, aria for alto with recorder obbligato and, continuo:

> <u>Leget euch dem Heiland unter,</u>   Prostrate yourselves before
> <u>Herzen die ihr christlich seid.</u>   the Savior you hearts which
>   are Christian.

This text, with its focusing on the downward gesture of prostrating oneself, is expressed by Bach in a recorder melody that has the following sequence:

The downward curve of the melody beautifully fits both the key word of the text (unterlegen) and the instrument.
    Even more vivid than this sighing characteristic of the recorder are its many associations with pastoral images. In the cantata literature, these images branch into two streams. One relates to the religious metaphor of the people as a flock of sheep and the Lord as the Shepherd. In this metaphor, the Lord guards His people, protects them, and watches over them. The flock is secure in the knowledge that they have a Faithful Shepherd.

> 208/9, aria for soprano, two recorders and continuo:
> <u>Schafe köonen sicher weiden</u>   Sheep may safely graze
> <u>wo ein guter Hirte wacht.</u>   where a good Shepherd
>   watches.

The gently bleating sounds of the recorders combine with the utterly simple melody of the soprano to create an unforgettable effect. Even more striking are the first two movements of <u>Cantata 175</u>.

> 175/1, recitative for tenor, three recorders and continuo:
> <u>Er rufet seinen Schafen mit Namen</u>   He calls His sheep by
> <u>und führet sie hinaus.</u>   name and leads them out.

> 175/2, an aria for alto, three recorders, and continuo:

> <u>Komm leite mich,</u>   Come lead me,
> <u>es sehnet sich</u>   it longs my spirit
> <u>mein Geist af grüner Weide.</u>   for green pastures.

Once again the sound of the recorders provides an indelible musical image, underlining both the Scriptural quotation of the recitative and the expressive, meditative character of the aria.

The other stream of pastoral images relates to the Nativity. The birth of Jesus in a manger with farm animals all around has created a very persistent flow of pastoral music from many Baroque composers, especially connected with Christmas. Bach created his own Nativity music using the recorders in a secular work. The slow movement of the Brandenburg Concerto No. 4 is a Nativity piece, even though it is not designated as such. There is a third association of the recorder that plays an even deeper role in the cantata music, and that is the association of the recorder sound with funerals. Three examples of this writing will be cited here.

161/1, aria for alto, with two recorders and continuo:
Komm. du süsse Todesstunde. Come, sweet hour of death.

Two features of the recorder writing relate to the text and help depict it. The parallel sixths and thirds express sweetness, and the groups of two notes under the slur, creating descending couplets, give a sighing or mournful character that tempers the sound. Cantata 106, Gottes Zeit ist die allerbeste Zeit, is a funeral cantata. It begins with an orchestral sinfonia which, of course, has no text. However, this sinfonia serves the role of introducing the subject matter of the entire cantata. In such moments Bach produces a musical utterance more vivid than the language of words. It may not be as precise or as delimiting a language, but it serves to create a wider resonance for the subject. The recorders play both an expressive role in the sinfonia and a symbolic one. In effect, they tell the listeners that they are at a funeral.

127/3, aria for soprano, oboe obbligato, two recorders,
    strings, and continuo:

Die Seele ruht in Jesu Händen wenn Erde diesen Leib bedeckt. Ach, ruft mich bald ihr Sterbeglocken, ich bin zum Sterben unerschrocken, weil mich mein Jesus wieder weckt.	The soul rests in Jesus' hands when earth covers this body. Ah, call me soon, you deathbells, I am unafraid to die for my Jesus will wake me again.

In this great aria of overwhelmingly beautiful melodic writing, the recorders play a relatively modest role. They are assigned a persistent figure of repeated tones that goes through the entire piece. The solo oboe, on the other hand, plays one of the most haunting and tragically rhapsodic lines one can imagine. When the soprano enters, as a partner to the oboe, the text speaks of the yearning of the soul for death and union with God. The bass line is very spare, reduced to pizzicato beats

every half measure. When the strings enter, late in the piece, they play
a series of bell sounds coinciding with the reference in the text to
death bells.   The composition exists, then, on various levels, both
representational and allegorical.   The allegorical side treats death in
orthodox Lutheran terms as a longed-for and blessed state, which leaves
behind the misery and suffering of earthly existence.   The representational level, on the other hand, pictures a funeral.   The recorders,
whose sounds are heard first, tell this. This level tells of sadness, of
mourning, and of terror, normal human reactions to death and funerals.
It speaks of concrete details, the earth covering the body and the sound
of bells (which announced the death of church members in Leipzig).   The
listeners are taken on a journey in which their souls are occupied with
thoughts of infinity, yet at the same time they are anchored in the
present. The recorders serve this anchoring function. Their distinctive
sounds tell us where we are and never let us forget it.

The Traverso in Bach Cantatas

If we perform the same kind of study for the flute music that we did
for the recorder, we discover a contrast in the range of expressive purposes that the instrument is called on to serve. The traverso is an ath-
lete, a virtuoso, with a penchant for vivid decoration.   If the recorder
speaks with a gentle and sad nature, the flute is generally more cheerful
and forthcoming. Cantata 94/1 is a striking mini-concerto for flute with
orchestra and chorus in D major. The chorus sings all the phrases of the
chorale Was frag ich nach der Welt, separated by orchestral interludes;
the voice of the flute is almost never still. It is a spirit of joy and
energy that pervades the score.
The "Polonaise" of the famous Suite in B Minor for flute and string
orchestra with continuo is another example of such a treament.   In the
Double section of this movement the main theme is played by the bass
voices while the flute plays rings around the melody, decorating it in
the most joyous way imaginable.
One of the most athletic flute parts in the cantata literature is
113/5, an aria for tenor with flute and continuo.

Jesus nimmt die Sünder an;   Jesus accepts sinners;
süsses Wort, voll Trost und Leben. sweet Word, full of
                                    comfort and life.

The flute ritornello starts with a melody that fits the words of the
first line, "Jesus nimmt die Sünder an." This is a quotation from the
chorale which the singer is contemplating. He finds it a "sweet word,"
full of life. The flute line expresses all these shifts of joyous

emotion, expressing first of all sweetness, then comfort, and finally life (in a burst of speed). Bach's way of showing this is to use three different levels of decoration.

Another characteristic flute expression in the aria literature of the Bach cantatas is found in a group of pieces that I call the er, pieces.

102/5:

Erschrecke doch,	Be frightened,
du allzu sichre Seele!	you smug soul!

99/3:

Erschüttre dich nur nicht,	Waver not,
verzagte Seele!	despondent soul!

180/2:

Ermuntre dich,	Arouse yourself,
dein Heiland klopft!	your Savior knocks!

All three of these pieces are for tenor with flute and continuo, all have very active flute parts, and all are in the imperative mode. Merely to think of the recorder in this kind of music is to see the difference that Bach perceived in the natures of these two instruments. The recorder is more passive, the flute more active. The recorder may express the sadness in its soul and invite you to share it, but the flute can speak to you, exhort you, and move you to act.

There is still another side to the flute that Bach perceived. He created a special niche for the traverso in which is found its most beautiful and profound music. I call this the hovering state. In these pieces the flute is called on to depict an inspired yet unstable state of trembling ecstasy. The feeling is of being not on the ground but suspended somewhere above it. The melodies are active and decorative, but the downbeats are not arrived at solidly. There are many suspensions.

249a/4, aria for soprano, flute, and continuo:

Hunderttausend Schmeicheleien   A hundred thousand
                                       flatteries

wallen jetzt in meiner Brust.   are now surging in
                                       my breast.

The music of this piece is found in the Easter Oratorio, but the
original words are part of a wedding cantata. The original words (given
above) suit the music better.

St. Matthew Passion/58, aria for soprano, flute, two oboes da
caccia:

Aus Liebe will mein Heiland sterben   Out of love will my
                                        Savior die.

This St. Matthew Passion aria is, of course, very well known and is
always memorable even in great performances of the entire work. It is
the only piece in the monumental structure that has no continuo. The
soprano and flute are accompanied by two oboes da caccia; there is no
keyboard and no supporting cello or bass. The lowest voice is the second
oboe. In a masterful dramatic touch, Bach places this piece of naive,
childlike heartbreak into the midst of earthy and turbulent sections re-
lating to the trial and death of Jesus.

100/4 Aria for soprano, flute, and continuo:

Was Gott thut, dass ist wohlgetan   What God does, that
                                        is well done.

A curious fact: all three of the above mentioned pieces share a
harmonic progression of a descending bass line over which the flute line
hovers.

151/1, aria for soprano with flute,
Süsser Trost, mein Jesus kommt,

strings and continuo:
Sweet comfort, my
Jesus comes

Jesus wird an itzt geboren!
Herz und Seele freuet sich,
denn mein liebster Gott hat mich
nun zum Himmel auserkoren.

Jesus now is born!
Heart and soul rejoice,
for my dearest God has
chosen me now for Heaven.

This aria may be the most beautiful of all the flute pieces in the cantata
literature. The first two lines are part of a Molto Adagio that is a
lullaby for the newborn infant. The last three lines are part of a
vivace section that glitters with activity. Both sides of the flute's
potential are shown. The musical illustration shows the entrance of the
soprano and the flute part that accompanies it. Notice the doubling and
the weaving in and out. It is truly a garland of ecstatic decorations.

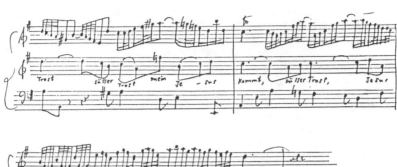

There are still some puzzles connected with Bach and the traverso. The
one that fascinates me the most is, what accounts for the intermittent
nature of Bach's use of the traverso? The flute appears in only about a
quarter of the Leipzig cantatas.

We must bear in mind that there could not have been many skilled
traversists in Germany in the 1720s. When the celebrated French traversist, Buffardin, came to Dresden in 1715, he was the only traversist in
Germany. Now it is undoubtedly true that the popularity of the instrument grew by leaps and bounds. One need only recall that Buffardin's
student, Johann Joachim Quantz, became the private flute teacher of
Frederick the Great and the music director of his court. The social
status (if nothing else) of flute playing was as high as it could be by
the 1740s.

To return to Bach in Leipzig, however,--when he wrote a traverso
part in a cantata there was usually an important obbligato part in an
aria. The writing for the flute in the cantatas is quite demanding. Is
it possible that Bach had a skilled flutist only some of the time? The
new dating of the Bach cantatas, which shows how much intense compositional activity went on in a short space of time (the first two or three
years after Bach arrived in Leipzig), places the flute cantatas in a very
striking sequence. It would appear that there was a skilled flutist, X,
who started to work for Bach on the seventh Sunday after Trinity in the
year 1723. This is the date of the first performance of Cantata 107.
Flute solos appear fairly regularly in the cantata from that date onward
for about half a year and then they stop. Did X leave? How did Bach
manage without X when the cantatas with flute solos were repeated in
subsequent years? We know of one case where a very difficult flute solo
was crossed out by Bach and recopied as a violin solo (101/2).

Isn't it tantalizing to think that Bach might have used the traverso more in his cantatas if he had had a reliable and competent player
more of the time? And, finally, who was X ?

3

An Odd Couple: J. S. Bach and A. S. Huxley

Sister Ann Edward Bennis

What could possibly connect the seventeenth century master of sacred song, J. S. Bach, with Aldous Huxley, the twentieth century master of social satire?   One connection is evident in a Huxley novel.   Huxley (1894-1963), a prolific writer and brilliant wit, had an encyclopedic mind with a rich knowledge of musical compositions. He delights in discussing music, as seen in his book of essays, Music At Night, 1931, and in several of his novels.

Of the novel, Point Counter Point (1928), Huxley writes that he based his thinking and his forms on Bach's contrapuntal techniques. This claim is obvious in the general structure of Point Counter Point and very specifically, in its first four chapters. They center on Bach's Suite in B-Minor.

The opening chapters of the novel are set in the music room of a large estate named Tantamount Hall. We are listening to a concert. The captive audience sits, enduring the orchestra; some guests are squirming, some gesturing, others whispering. One man stage-whispers, "This is like being in a deaf-and-dumb asylum." p. 27. Lady Edward Tantamount hears the comment and flaps her ostrich-fan at the whisperer. Meanwhile, the musicians keep playing Bach's Suite.

This B-Minor Suite becomes the focus of the novel's next chapters, where Huxley creates a verbal parallel of Bach's text.

In a succinct, witty, yet always reverent commentary, the words let us experience the Suite. We hear it, we feel it, we know it. We then read a satiric description of the conductor. He is "bending in swan-like undulation and tracing luscious arabesques on the air with his waving arms . . . fiddlers and cellists scrape at his bidding, while Bach's meditation fills the air". p. 27. Huxley then introduces the first movement of a suite, the Largo, with its slow, majestic rhythms: "In the opening Largo, John Sebastian made a statement: 'there are grand things in the world, noble things; there are men born kingly; there are conquerors and heroes'". p. 27.

(I digress to mention that if, while we are reading Huxley's words on the Suite, we listen to a recording of the work, we can feel the stateliness and grandeur of the Largo and the changing moods of the movements that follow. The listening can be a spiritual experience, a religious one, as Huxley confirms in a letter he wrote forty years after Point Counter Point. A segment of the letter concludes this essay.)

After the Largo, Huxley reflects on the next section, the Fugue, or "fugal Allegro." Here, says the author, "You seem to have found the truth. Clear, definite, unmistakable, it is announced by the violins."p. 27. The it here, or the truth, indicates what in a fugue is called the subject--in ordinary parlance, the theme or the motif. In Bach's Suite, this subject repeats and interweaves among the instruments--the flute, the cello, and the violins. The fugue's subject, the it, becomes a palpable reality for Huxley. He says: "You hold it; it slips out of your grasp to come back in a new aspect with the cellos, and comes again in a vibrating air column". p. 27. ("Air column" is Huxley's euphemism for the flute.)

In the Suite we hear the subject, or the theme, singly at first, then interlinked with stringed instruments, and finally with the flute.

Through each movement, Bach continues the contrapuntal progression, the interweaving. Huxley comments on this technique in two direct, brief passages that can serve the nonmusician with simple definitions of counterpoint. In the first passage, we listen to the orchestra and "the parts live their separate lives; their paths cross, they combine for a moment to create a seemingly final and perfect harmony, only to break apart again". p. 27. Huxley's other passage dramatizes the contrapuntal art when he has the instruments arguing: "Each part is alone and separate and individual. ´I am I. The world revolves around me´, asserts the violin. ´Round me´, calls the cello.´ Round me´ the flute insists". p. 28. Huxley responds to the Suite's next movement, the Rondeau. "Here is a particular part and John Sebastian puts the case." (Note how Huxley enjoys the homey and familiar first names instead of the name universally used--Bach.)

The orchestra begins the Rondeau, which for Huxley is "exquisitely and simply melodious." Then the author indulges in a highly personal fantasizing, one that might be rejected by Bach himself or by Bach lovers and scholars, who know that a rondeau is a traditional, stylized French dance. Huxley knows this, too, but he expresses what he feels, not what he knows. In a dreamy, romantic moment, he muses on the Rondeau: "It is a young girl singing to herself, tenderly mournful. A young girl singing among the hills with the clouds drifting overhead." p. 28. Huxley calls these imaginings his thoughts. We call them fancies or feelings. The thoughts continue as Huxley enters the movement after the Rondeau. This is a Sarabande. In contrast to the sprightly, jaunty Rondeau, the Sarabande is like a dignified dance whose melody is easily embellished and decorated. For Huxley, a sarabande is "a slow and lovely meditation on the beauty (in spite of squalor), the profound good (in spite of evil), the oneness (in spite of bewildering diversity) of the world." p. 28. Huxley follows these moralistic contrasts with a rhetorical question about the music: "Is it illusion or is it the revelation of profound truth? Who knows?" p. 28.

After pages of concentration on the Suite itself, we are suddenly jolted back to the concert. Huxley has kept us so absorbed in the music that we almost forgot the audience. Again, as in the opening, a stage whisper intrudes on the orchestra. "This music is getting tedious. Will it last much longer?" p. 28. A few audible murmurs follow, with a chorus of "sh-sh-s." Huxley counters the boredom with one of his kudos for Bach, calling him a poet: "Bach, the poet, meditated on truth and beauty." p. 28. This oscillation of the audience versus the music, of life versus art, offers again a sample of contrapuntal texture.

With the melodies pulling against one another, Chapter 2 ends. The scene changes in Chapter 3. We are in the mansion, four flights upstairs in a science laboratory, where Lord Edward and a helper are busily dissecting a small bug. Huxley describes the experiment with microscopic detail. Soon "fragments of the B-Minor Suite came floating up from the Great Hall to the ears of the men, but they were too busy to hear it." p. 36. Later, when a "pattern of melody traced itself up into the silence," Lord Edward heard it and whispered, "Bach?" p. 38.

Some comic close-ups follow, telling how the music kept bouncing around inside Edward's ear and how he sighed ecstatically, "Bach! His eyes lit up." Here, in another instance of counterpoint, Huxley repeats

almost verbatim his sentence about the Rondeau: "A young girl is singing
to herself in solitude under the floating clouds" and "Lord Edward begins
to lust irrepressibly for Bach.   Then he goes downstairs to listen."
p. 38.

Chapter 4 of Huxley's novel opens with the last dance of Bach's
Suite.   This dance is a rollicking, jig-type badinage--a light happy
movement in contrast to the opening Largo.   In describing the dance, Huxley uses the lingo of mathematics--a touch germane in discussing Bach,
who is consistently precise, measured, and exact, even though his glorious notes flow smoothly and easily.

The concert concludes with Huxley's staccato math metaphors: "Eucli-
dean axioms made holiday. . . . Arithmetic held a wild saturnalia. Al-
gebra cut capers.   The music ended in an orgy of mathematical merry-mak-
ing. . .Torrents of pent-up chatter broke loose." p. 42.   In this releas-
ed chatter the guests talk of food, gossip and other trivia, with not a
hint of the awe, the inspiration, and the silence that can fill a heart
exposed to the beauty of Bach.   In these passages, Huxley shows his con-
summate gift of satire, mingling the serious and the silly, the sensitive
and the crass, the grand and the lowly.

By Chapter 5, the Bach music is over, but the Bach structures continue through the 500 pages of the novel.   Pitted against one another are
contrasts of past and present, youth and age, life and death, love and
hate.   This contrapuntal technique also marks Huxley's style; for example, in the lab when sounds of music are minutely delineated inside
Edward's ear as he continues exploring his insect.

Huxley's use of the Suite in B-Minor is a daring analogy, and a
risky one.   We humans can see many things at one time; we can hear many
things at one time; but can we read many levels at one time? Not easily.
But somehow Huxley forces us to do this in Point Counter Point, which
consciously and deliberately adapts to Bach's musical technique.   At
times in the novel, Huxley manages to have three conversations interpene-
trating, like the Suite's violin and cello and flute.   Also, he can in-
terweave several themes, smoothly creating a network of parallels and
contrasts, similar to Bach's method.   Thus, in Huxley, his daring analogy
holds.

We conclude with a segment from the Huxley letter mentioned herein.
He wrote it in 1955, forty years after Point Counter Point (1928). Huxley
had been ill and the drug LSD was one of the medications prescribed.   The
letter to his doctor tells of taking LSD and listening to Bach's Suite in
B-Minor.   The account is somewhat clinical, yet it is transcendent, con-
fessional, and witty, echoing the emotions that Huxley created in Point
Counter Point:

> I played the Bach B-Minor Suite and the experience was over-
> whelming. . . Bach was a revelation. The tempo of the pieces
> did not end: they went on for centuries, with a manifestation
> of perpetual creation--an impression of the essential all-
> rightness of the universe . . . Who on earth was John Sebast-
> ian? Certainly not the old gentleman with sixteen children
> in a stuffy religious environment! Rather, an enormous mani-
> festation of the Other--of God--made available through the
> intellect and the senses and the emotions . . . Listening to
> the B-Minor Suite brought me a direct, unmediated understand-
> ing of the divine nature p. 779.

REFERENCES

Huxley, Aldous, Point Counter Point.   Modern Library, N.Y. 1928 p.
27, 28, 36, 38, 42.
Letters of Aldous Huxley, Grover Smith, ed. Harper and Row, N.Y.
1969 p. 779.

4

Hemiola in the
Eighteenth Century

Vincent Corrigan

Hemiola is a general term used to indicate the ratio three=to=two, and
its musical applications are varied. It may refer to the interval of the
fifth, whose frequencies and string lengths show the 3:2 relationship.
It is also used to describe triplets. (1) As a notational term, it indicates coloration, particularly the use of blackened notes in tempus
perfectum. (2) During the late eighteenth and early nineteenth centuries,
it even indicated the time signatures 5/4 and 5/8. (3) However, it is now
used most often to describe metric shifts that occur when, for instance,
two dotted half notes are replaced by three half notes: d.d. = d d d.
     The result, in this case, is a shift in meter from 6/4 to 3/2, char-
acteristic of the French courante. This is only the simplest example,
however; in eighteenth century musical sources, hemiola is widely used
and appears in much more complicated ways.   Studies dealing with hemiola
in the works of individual composers have pointed the way to a more comprehensive view of the subject, but questions still remain about how
eighteenth century musicians thought of hemiola and how they used the
technique in their compositions. (4)
     The definitions in dictionaries of the period are curiously antiqua-
ted. (5) They describe hemiola in terms of coloration, and use breves
and semibreves to illustrate the patterns.   Two types of hemiola are
recognized.   In the major hemiola, three blackened, imperfect breves
replace two normal perfect breves; in the minor hemiola, the altered note
value is the semibreve.   Analogues to these two types occur in the
musical sources. In some cases, two measures of simple triple meter, for
instance 3/4, are combined to form one measure twice as long, in this
case 3/2. In others, the accentual pattern within a measure of compound
duple meter (e.g. 6/8) is altered to produce a measure of simple triple
meter (3/4). In this discussion I will use the term major hemiola to
describe situations in which two measures are combined into one. The
term minor hemiola will refer to hemiola that operates within a measure.
Table 4.1 lists the most frequently encountered metric shifts, and Example 4.1 provides some characteristic passages. (6)

T 4.1

Major hemiola	Minor hemiola
2 x 3/4 -- 3/2	6/4 -- 3/2
2 x 3/8 -- 3/4	6/8 -- 3/4

Example 4.1

a. G.F. Hadel: Menuetto in G Minor (Second Collection, 1733), mm. 14-16

b. D. Scarlatti: Sonata in C Minor (K. 226), mm. 63-65

c. F. Couperin: 27th Ordre, Les Chinois, mm. 15-16

d. J.S. Bach: English Suite No. 1 (BWV 806), Gigue, mm. 15-16

The major hemiola appears in Examples 4.1a and b. In both cases the primary accent in the second measure is suppressed. In Example 4.1a: this is achieved by the use of a tie and by the harmonic progression. In Example 4.1b, a rest replaces the primary accent. The minor hemiola appears in Examples 4.1c and 4.1d. In both cases two secondary accents replace the one that was expected, and in both cases this is achieved by the harmonic progression and by agogic stress.

Other metric shifts exist, but are less frequently seen. Perhaps because most of them are rare, they have a remarkable effect on the listener's perception of pulse. Table 4.2 lists these exceptional shifts, and Example 4.2 provides some representative passages.

T 4.2

Major hemiola	Minor hemiola
2 x 3/2 -- 3/1	3/2 -- 6/4
	3/4 -- 6/8
	3/8 -- 6/16

Example 4.2

a. F. Couperin: 3rd Ordre, Courante No. 2. mm 7-8

b. J. S. Bach: Ouverture (BWV 831), Courante, mm. 1-2

c. G. B. Sammartini: <u>Symphony in C Major</u> (JC 7), 1st movement, mm. 56-62

d. J. P. Rameau: <u>Ouverture</u> to <u>Pygmalion</u>, mm. 52-55

In Example 4.2a; the minor hemiola is used to produce the metric juxtaposition characteristic of the French courante. Another courante is shown in Example 4.2b, but here the major hemiola 3/2--3/1 is used in the bass line. In Example 4.2c, the metric shift is achieved by agogic accents in the first violin part. Example 4.2d deserves special comment. It would seem that composers often treated the 6/8 measure as a combination of two 3/8 units, each of which could show the minor hemiola 3/8-- 6/16. This, at least, is the simplest explanation.

Many writers have emphasized what they call the closing hemiola, (Schlusshemiole). (7) This ubiquitous device is found in the measure or two before any cadence, internal as well as final. Both the major and minor hemiolas can be used in this way; in fact, Example 4.1 consists exclusively of closing hemiolas. Cadence points, then, are preferred positions for hemiola patterns. It is further maintained that the closing hemiola has the effect of a ritard, and thus the generalization has been made that eighteenth century composers used hemiola to slow the pulse at cadence points. This is not a safe assumption; the true situation is somewhat different, as can be seen from the following considerations.

In a normal hemiola pattern, three shortened note values replace two normal equivalent note values. Because the substituted notes are one third shorter, they are faster by the relationship three=to=two. When normal values reassert themselves, the pulse slows down by one-third. Consider Examples 4.1b. and d. Most of the time the pulse is heard to fall on the dotted quarter note. At cadences the pulse shifts to the quarter note, and is heard to speed up. Now consider Examples 4.1a and c. In both, the equivalent note values are the dotted half note and the half note, and of course the half note is one third faster. However, it is often more convenient for listeners to pulse the quarter note in pieces such as these. If a quarter note pulse is maintained through the hemiola, it will not change in speed; rather, pulses will be heard to fall into groups of two rather than groups of three. A ritard only arises if the listener stops pulsing the quarter note and begins instead to pulse the half note. That is, a ritard comes about only when nonequivalent note values are pulsed. However, there is no indication that nonequivalent note values were ever considered in this way. As a result, it is not safe to assume that hemiola was used to slow the pulse at cadences. In fact, the pulse normally speeds up.

Furthermore, it is not safe to assume that hemiola appears exclusively at cadence points, or that the closing hemiola is especially significant. Most composers were much more ingenious in their treatment of meter. Example 4.3 provides passages illustrating what might be called the opening hemiola.

Example 4.3

a. J. S. Bach: Parita No. 4 (BWV 828), Menuet, mm. 1-2

b. J. S. Bach: Parita No. 4 (BWV 828, Gigue, mm. 1-2

c. J. S. Bach: Partita No. 5 (BWV 829), Corrente, mm. 1-2

d. J.S. Bach: Toccata and Fugue (BWV 564), Fugue, mm. 1-9

In the first three passages, the major hemiola is used to obscure the notated meter. Not until at least the third measure of each piece is the true meter clear. In Example 4.3d, the true meter is heard only in the seventh and eighth measures. In the other measures the minor hemiola creates the effect of 3/4. It might be noted that Example 4.3b adds another metric transformation to those already listed. Here the major hemiola combines two measures of 9/16 into one measure of 18/16.

The description of hemiola in terms of its position within a piece is ultimately misleading and futile, because hemiola can occur anywhere and can be maintained for extended periods of time. One example may suffice to illustrate this point. Example 4.4 shows a portion of the second half of the <u>Two-Part Invention in E Major.</u> Here six measures of 3/8 are combined into three measures of 3/4 by means of the major hemiola.

As is evident in the preceding examples, hemiola patterns can result in multimeters if the meter changes appear in succession, as happens throughout Example 4.1. Alternately, hemiola can produce polymeters when two different meters are used simultaneously. Polymeters can be seen in Examples 4.2b and c. In both cases the metric contrasts are presented in a straightforward manner. However, hemiola can also be combined with syncopation to produce structures of far greater complexity. Syncopation is meant here in its mensural sense, as the separation of the units of a perfection by the insertion of one or more perfections. (8) Mensural notation could express this complexity explicitly by mean of coloration; eighteenth century notation could not, and consequently, many interpretations are conjectural. Examples 4.5 shows apparently clear-cut examples of this technique.

Example 4.4

J. S. Bach: <u>Invention No. 6 in E Major</u> (BWV 777), mm. 33-38

a. D. Scarlatti: <u>Sonata in B-flat</u> (K. 228), mm. 46-51

b. J. S. Bach Ouverture (BWV 831), Courante, mm. 20-22

c. D. Scarlatti: Sonata in G Major (K. 125), mm. 11-19

Example 4.5

        In Example 4.5 one measure of 3/8 has been inserted between the
first and second quarter note units of the major hemiola. The opposite
approach appears in Example 4.5b. Here the major hemiola has been
inserted between the first and second half notes of a 3/2 measure.   In
Example 4.5c, a major hemiola begins in measure 13. After its fourth
eighth note, there is inserted a measure of 3/8, a measure of 3/4, and
another measure of 3/8. Only after this interruption is the hemiola that
was begun in measure 13 completed.
        One of the finest examples of metric manipulation can be found in
the last movement of Bach's Gamba Sonata in D Major (BWV 1028). The
movement is based on three motives, shown in Example 4.6a, each of which
implies a different meter. The first motive reinforces 6/8, while the
second is to be heard in 3/4. The third motive is heard, not as two
measure of 6/8, but as four measures of 6/16. These motives are combined
in various ways throughout the movement to produce both multimeters and
polymeters. In addition, three passages (mm. 8-16, 66-69, 118-125)
employ syncopation in conjunction with hemiola. A portion of the last of

these passages is given in Example 4.6b in what appears to be its true
metric guise.

Example 4.6

J. S. Bach: <u>Sonata for Gamba and Harpischord</u> BWV 1028), Allegro
a.   5-6; 1-2; 14-15

b.   mm.121-125

Hemiola, as practiced in the eighteenth century, has its roots in
mensural notation, and many of its characteristics can be related to
those of earlier centuries despite the enormous changes in the notational
system.   Furthermore, the terms that most precisely describe the metric
transformations that take place are those of mensural notation.   Table
4.3 lists all the metric shifts that may be subsumed under the concept of
hemiola, together with their appropriate mensural descriptions.

T 4.3

MAJOR HEMIOLA

Modus Imperfectum	Modus Perfectum
1. Tempus perfectum, prolatio perfecta	Tempus imperfectum, prolatio perfecta
a. 2 x 9/8	18/8 (3 x 6/8)
b. 2 x 9/16	18/16 (3 x 6/16)

2. Tempus perfectum, prolatio   Tempus imperfectum,
    imperfecta   prolatio imperfecta

    a. 2 x 3/2   3/1 (3 x 2/2)
    b. 2 x 3/4   3/2 (3 x 2/4)
    c. 2 x 3/8   3/4 (3 x 2/8)

MINOR HEMIOLA

3. Tempus imperfectum, prolatio   Tempus perfectum,
    perfecta   prolatio imperfecta
    a. 6/4   3/2
    b. 6/8   3/4

4. Tempus perfectum, prolatio   Tempus imperfectum,
    imperfecta   prolatio perfecta

    a. 3/2   6/4
    b. 3/4   6/8
    c. 3/8   6/16

All the time signatures found in the preceding examples are included here. In addition, the Table provides one other metric shift that may be expected to occur, item 1a. A particularly clear example of this shift can be found in Bach´s Prelude in E-flat Major (WTC II, mm. 67-68). Two measures of 9/8 are combined to make one measure of 18/8, or rather three measure of 6/8. Furthermore, the second of the 6/8 units is itself subject to the minor hemiola, producing one unit of 3/4 (Example 4.7).

Example 4.7

J. S. Bach: Prelude in E-flat major (WTC II, BWV 876), mm. 66-68

There is ample evidence to suggest that hemiola was a very popular device in the early eighteenth century, and that it was used consciously to produce a great deal of metric turmoil. However, despite the vitality in its application, hemiola was generally considered an old-fashioned technique. It is clear that the most precise descriptions of hemiola are also the most antiquated. In any case, hemiola had all but disappeared by the latter part of the century. Replacing it was a rhythmic style that was simpler, less ambiguous, but metrically focused, much as a simpler, diatonic, tonally focused harmonic style replaced the earlier chromaticism. When hemiola reappeared in the works of Robert Schumann and Johannes Brahms, its mensural associations were all but forgotten. Thus, hemiola in the eighteenth century represents one of the last vestiges of mensural thinking, and its passing signaled the death of a fundamental procedure for the measurement of time.

NOTES

1.   See Michael B. Collins, "The Performance of Sesquialtera and Hemiola in the 16th Century," Journal of the American Musicological Society 17 (1964):   5-28; see also Michael B. Collins, "The Performance of Triplets in the 17th and 18th Centuries," Journal of the American Musicological Society 19 (1966): 281-328.

2.   Willi Apel, The Notation of Polyphonic Music--900-1600 5th ed., rev. with commentary (Cambridge, Mass.: Medieval Academy of America, 1953), p. 131.

3.   Jean-Jacques Rousseau, Dictionnaire de Musique, Nouvelle Edition (1766), s.v."Hemiola"; and Heinrich Christoph Koch, Musikalisches Lexikon (1802), s.v. "Hemiola."

4.   Karel Philippus Bernet-Kempers, "Hemiolenrhythmik bei Mozart," in Festschrift Helmut Osthoff zum 65. Geburtstage, ed. Lothar Hoffmann-Erbrecht and Helmut Hucke (Tutzing: Hans Schneider Verlag, 1961), pp. 155-61;   Werner Tell, "Die Hemiole bei Bach," Bach-Jahrbuch 39 (1951-52): 47-53;   H.H. Wintersgill, "Handel's Two-Length Bar," Music and Letters 17 (1936): 1-12.

5.   In addition to the dictionaries cited above (note 3), see Sebastien de Brossard, Dictionaire de Musique (1703), s.v. "Hemiolia"; James Grassineau, A Musical Dictionary (1740), s.v. "Hemiolia"; Johann Gottfried Walter, Musicalisches Lexicon (1732), "Hemiolia"; Kurzgefasstes musicalisches Lexicon (1737), s.v. "Hemiolia."

6.   In this and all subsequent tables, the notated time signature is given on the left-hand side of each column.

7.   Hans Hering, "Die Dynamik in Joh. Seb. Bachs Klaviermusik," Bach-Jahrbuch 37 (1949-50): 71;   see also Tell, "Die Hemiole," p. 48.

8.   See Apel, Notation, p. 395ff on the definition of syncopation.

5

The "Unravelling" of Schoenberg's Bach

John J. Daverio

I

The prose writings of Arnold Schoenberg are characterized by a markedly polemical tone. This is even evident--one might say, especially evident --in Schoenberg's often idiosyncratic commentaries on the music of the eighteenth and nineteenth century German masters. On one hand, Schoenberg was anxious to justify his own radical musical procedures by finding precedents for them in the tradition that he so revered. Thus, he asserted that Bach, whose Fuga XXIV in B Minor from Book 1 of Das Wohltemperirte Clavier (The Well-Tempered Clavier) was based on a subject containing all twelve pitches of the chromatic scale, was "the first composer with twelve tones."(1) At the same time, Schoenberg's reinterpretation of the past was not without genuine analytical insights that have since

Perhaps none of his technical categories has received as much attention as the one he called developing variation, and associated with the homophonic-melodic style of composition (that is, music from the period of Viennese Classicism to that of Mahler and Strauss). According to this principle, "variation of the features of a basic unit produces all the thematic formulations which provide for fluency, contrast, variety, logic and unity, on the one hand, and character, mood, expression, and every needed differentiation, on the other hand--thus elaborating the idea of the piece."(2) Most recently, the concept of developing variation has been employed as a means of coming to terms with the intense motivic work characteristic of the mature compositions of Johannes Brahms.(3)

What has not been much noted is that, for Schoenberg, developing variation formed only one aspect of a larger, dual-natured principle. He coupled developing variation with the technique that governed contrapuntal works, or, as he called it, "unravelling."(4) While developing variation involves the linear elaboration of a motivic idea, unravelling takes as its point of departure a combinative unit, that is, several ideas presented simultaneously. The pairing of the complementary ideas, Entwicklung (vertical development) and Abwicklung (horizontal unravelling) is a theme to which Schoenberg returned constantly in his prose writings,(5) for it was the interaction of horizontal elaboration and vertical combination that he pinpointed as the primary agent of music-historical change.(6) Although he maintained that these two notions were diametrically opposed to one another,(7) Schoenberg was, in fact, most fascinated by the possiblity of fusing them.(8) Indeed, he hoped to achieve just such a fusion of the vertical and horizontal dimensions in his own music,(9) and was naturally drawn to those works from the past in which a similar interpenetration of Entwicklung and Abwicklung was in evidence.(10)

My own aim in the present essay is twofold. First, I will examine

the element of Schoenberg´s dialectic pair that has received little
attention, the contrapuntal concept of unravelling. Not surprisingly,
Schoenberg suggested that this was the principle that guided Bach´s
fugues, and his idea is worth investigating further. Second, an examination of Bach´s fugal technique from Schoenberg´s point of view will
demonstrate that an analysis based solely on the unravelling idea produces a decidely one-sided picture of Bach´s art. (Likewise, any consideration of the music of Brahms or any other composer of the homophonic
era from the standpoint of developing variation alone will be equally
incomplete.) The richness of Bach´s fugal writing is rather the result of
the fusion of developing variation and contrapuntal unravelling to
produce what Schoenberg called "musical prose."(11)   Thus, it was the
presence of simultaneous development in Bach´s fugues that so impressed
Schoenberg (and not the more simplistic notion of the conflict between
harmony and counterpoint), and a closer look at this process may be of
some help in defining the technical aspects of Bach´s fugal works.

II

It is significant that Schoenberg´s most often-quoted definition of
developing variation should have occurred in his 1950 essay on Bach,
where it was coupled with a complementary account of the unravelling
principle. His remarks deserve to be quoted in full: Contrapuntal composition does not produce its material by development, but by a procedure
rather to be called unravelling. That is, a basic configuration or
combination taken asunder and reassembled in a different order contains
everything which will later produce a different sound than that of the
original formulation. Thus, a canon of two or more voices can be written
in one single line, yet furnishes various sounds. If multiple counter-
points are applied, a combination of three voices, invertible in the
octave, tenth and twelfth, offers so many combinations that even longer
pieces can be derived from it.(12)

Basic to the concept of unravelling is the notion that the theme of
a contapuntal work should remain fundamentally unchanged.(13)   If the
idea of, let us say, a fugue, hinges on the combination of several distinct motivic strands, then the subjection of one of these elements to
the process of development (which Schoenberg viewed as the generation of
new material in the horizontal direction) would of course destroy the
connections set out in the "basic configuration."(14) Thus, a fugue does
not produce contrast by developing new ideas, but by the addition of one
or more main voices (Hauptstimmen) to what appears to be given out, in
the opening measures, as a single main voice.(15)   In a fugue, the basic
combination frequently hinges on the simultaneous presentation of subject
and countersubject. Likewise, a linear entity may serve as the basis of
a combinative unit by being combined with itself in canon or stretto. In
addition, as Schoenberg often pointed out, the fashioning of the various
voices in terms of invertible counterpoint will allow for yet further
possible combinations.(16)   Perhaps the most striking aspect of the unravelling principle is Schoenberg´s avoidance of the more usual notion
that contrapuntal elaboration is a fundamentally linear process.(17)
Even the idea of imitation does not much come into play. Thus, the
linear quality, which seems of primary importance when an imitative work
is heard, is somewhat deceptive; for Schoenberg, the combinative aspect
is decisive.

In his essay on Bach, Schoenberg stated that he was led to formulate
his theory on the nature of contrapuntal technique through an examination
of those Bach fugues that appeared to eschew the more usual contrapuntal
complexities, and thus seemed "to correspond to the most superficial
concept of the several entrances of themes fleeing from one another."(18)
The unravelling principle was thus intended to shed light on the myster-

ies of fugal construction even in fugues where no mystery was obvious.
Schoenberg mentioned six fugues of this sort, all from Book 1 of the Well-
Tempered Clavier: Numbers 1, 3, 6, 9, and 17. (19)   Although each of
these works is, of course, highly distinctive in its own way, the special
peculiarities of Fuga VI in D Minor (Example 5.1) are such that it would
seem particularly appropriate for an examination from the Schoenbergian
point of view.

A discussion of Fuga VI based on traditional fugal theory and terminology will not get us very far. The material of mm. 3-4 in the top
voice (labelled as thematic fragments c and d in Example 5.2), for instance, appears at first to be treated as a countersubject.   Linear
statements of a and b (the subject) are more or less consistently coupled
with simultaneous statements of c and d until the appearance of the subject statement in the top voice at m. 13 (see Table 5.1).   While a5 and
c are presented simultaneously in m. 13, m. 14 brings together motive b5
(in the top voice), and, not d (as we might expect), but a7 (in the bass)
and aI2 (in the alto). As Table 5.1 makes clear, the following measures
present additional two-and three-motive combinations, many involving inversion, and none of which might have been predicted on the basis of the
regular layout of the opening fugal exposition (mm. 1-8) and its vertical
pairings of a and c, and b and d. (See, for instance, mm. 15-16, which
bring together various forms of a, b, and c; or mm. 17-18, which involve
a and d). Measure 5, which separates the first two subject statements in
the top and middle voices from that in the bass, presages to an extent
the various combinative capabilities of Bach´s four-measure theme in
stating b4 and c5 simultaneously. The same is true of m. 12, where aI5
and b are combined. Likewise, the unfolding of ever-new combinations
continues unabated in the second half of the fugue (labelled Part 2 in
Table 5.1).

The fundamental combination, that from which all future dispositions
are drawn, is stated in m. 3. Like the basic combination, that presented
in m. 4 (b and d) can be viewed as the enlivening of a simple intervallic
succession mainly through the application of appoggiature. The relationship of b and d to the basic motive pair can be clarified by reducing mm.
3-4 to their underlying intervallic pattern. (See Example 5.3).   Not
only is there a melodic correspondence between the last two beats of both
measures, but more important, the interval progression of both combinations is largely determined by the third (and its inversion, the sixth),
thus allowing for the subjection of each motivic pair to invertible
counterpoint at the octave.   All further two-motive combinations are
likewise traceable directly (or indirectly, through b and d) to the basic
pairing, a and c. The combination of a and d, which emphasizes the vertical intervals of a third and a sixth, is a clear derivative of a and c;
while a and b, and likewise b and c, bring together the slower harmonic/
intervallic rhythm of b and d with interval progressions closer to a and
c. In any case, the various contrapuntal maneuvers (the free combination
of two and three motives in original and inverted forms, the almost per-
vasive application of the technique of invertible counterpoint), all stem
from--and are made possible by--the prominence of the third and the sixth
as melodic and vertical intervals in the fundamental combination.

This fugue, then, is incredibly dense; that is, there is very little
free material. However, while this is characteristic of Bach´s fugues in
general, what makes Fuga VI so special is the rigor with which subsidiary
material is fashioned--largely through inversion--and the seeming ease
with which the inverted motive forms combine with the original ones. (The
range of combinations is, therefore, much wider than in the so-called
permutation fugues found in several of Bach´s Mühlhausen and Weimar cantatas, e.g., "Dein Alter sei wie deiner Jugend" from Cantata 71). Thus,
it was clearly the all-combinative property in works such as Fuga VI that
so impressed Schoenberg.

Just as the traditional notion of countersubject does not fully address the combinative aspects of Bach's fugue, so too the term subject fails to describe its basic thematic material. Thus, in m. 12 (following on the completion of the first episode), there is an entry in the bass that begins with the second measure of the subject, proceeds with the first measure of the countersubject, and only then provides the first measure of the subject (which proves to be a false entry). It is also difficult to consider the first four measures in the upper voice as a theme, for what four-measure theme could manage without its third measure (see mm. 17-19 and 39-41 in the bass), without its second measure (see mm. 35ff. in the upper voice), or with an extended pause between its third and fourth measures (see mm. 3-7 in the middle voice)? Rather, mm. 1-4 in the top voice form a thematic/motivic idea in the Schoenbergian sense, capable of elaboration in both the vertical and horizontal directions. They thus supply the basic configuration to which Schoenberg alluded in his definition of unravelling.

While the combinative properties of Bach's initial idea can be discussed in terms of contrapuntal principles, the horizontal unfolding of this idea involves the complementary technique of developing variation.(20)   As already noted, the idea is compressed by the elimination of one or more of its elements (see Table 5.1, mm. 5-6, b-c in the top voice); compressed versions are at times further altered by the presentation of individual motives in inversion (mm. 26-27 in the bass, a14-c5); or are expanded by the varied repetition of motivic units (mm. 35-40 in the upper voice);   and in some instances the entire idea is presented in expanded form (mm. 13-18 in the upper voice, and mm. 6-11 in the bass). A thoroughgoing transformation is given in Example 5.4, where an inversion of a and b proceeds to a variant of a transposed form of d; and then to two measures in which d appears in free inversion. (A similar technique is employed in the top voice, mm. 27-32.)

Likewise, the design of the fugue as a whole is not specifically contrapuntal, but rather is patterned after the homophonic form associated with the stylized dances of the High Baroque. It is cast in a binary form as clear as that in any of Bach's allemandes or gigues. Were we to imagine a central double bar, it would slice through the octave A at m. 21, which marks the only strong internal cadence (in the dominant, A minor), but at once is elided with the second, parallel half. This parallelism is made most obvious to the listener through the correspondence of the cadential measures in each half (see Example 5.5). Just as in most stylized dance movements, the closing measures of the second half repeat the cadential gesture of the first half in the tonic. However, a look at the boxed-in areas in Table 5.1 will readily show that the correspondence is more extensive. The vertical combinations in mm. 30-42 of the second half reproduce almost exactly the motivic material of mm. 9-20 in the first half (corresponding measures have been aligned in Table 5.1 for comparison). Of course, Bach varies the original material extensively. Motivic elements first presented in inversion recur in their original shape (cf. mm. 12 and 33) and vice versa (cf. mm. 9 and 30); in addition, transposition levels are altered to allow the second half to close in the tonic. While these alterations involve the developing variation principle, the vertical realignment of the motivic units (according to the principles of invertible counterpoint) clearly represents a variety of contrapuntal variation (cf. especially mm. 9-14 and 30-35 in Table 5.1).

With this final turn to contrapuntal procedures, my examination of the Fugue in D Minor comes full circle, and is indeed indicative of the dialectic that characterizes the work. Although the vertical and horizontal directions have been discussed separately, the technical richness of the fugue is a product of the continual interaction of opposed principles: At the same time that the initial melodic idea is being developed linearly, its separate motivic fragments are combined vertically to form an ever-changing array of contrapuntally unravelled units. Just as the unravelling technique provides the fugue with textural density and richness, the linear unfolding of the primarily homophonic form allows for what Schoenberg called "comprehensibility." Simultaneous elaboration in both directions gives rise to "musical prose."

III

In his essay "Brahms the Progressive," Schoenberg asserted that great musical art "must proceed to precision and brevity," thus tending toward a kind of "musical prose," that is, "a direct and straightforward presentation of ideas, without any patchwork, without mere padding and empty repetitions."(21)   Although he emphasized the importance of asymmetrical phrase structure as a result of prose-like construction, Schoenberg never clearly spelled out the technical means by which musical prose was to be produced.(22) Bach's fugue provides a clue, as do Schoenberg's comments on his own struggle toward the end of brevity in presentation. He claimed that in many of his early works (notably Verklärte Nacht, Op. 4, and the String Quartet in D Minor, Op. 7) he attempted to reach this goal by means of contrapuntal procedures, thus presenting in condensed fashion that which might otherwise be unfolded at greater length through developing variation.(23)   However, if the brevity characteristic of musical prose is to be achieved in part through contrapuntal combinations, Schoenberg also felt that a composer should strive for "comprehensibility."(24) He argued that comprehensibility was best ensured through repetition--not only exact repetition or sequence--but more especially through the inexact repetitions and elaborate transformations produced by developing variation.(25)   Thus, if musical prose results from the presentation of concise ideas in a comprehensible fashion, then it is produced by the dialectic play of contrapuntal unravelling and developing variation that I have noted in Bach's Fugue in D Minor.(26)

Ultimately, it was the contrast and fusion of seemingly opposed principles that would have made Bach a "modern" in Schoenberg's eyes. Although he denied that he ever intended to compare himself with Bach, Schoenberg made much of this very comparison in his essay "New Music, Outmoded Music, Style and Idea." What most intrigued him was the dialectic, not only in Bach's style, but also in his historical position, which Schoenberg, in turn, saw as comparable with his own. While Bach at once brought the contrapuntal era to a climax, and out of it created the technique of developing variation, so, too, would Schoenberg create something truly original out of the compositional principle of the homophonic era; that is, developing variation, and re-effect a fusion of linear elaboration and contrapuntal combination.(27)   His musical prose would be utterly "new," but at the same time firmly grounded in tradition.

Schoenberg would have been the first to admit that all of this tells us less about the nature of his music, than that it sheds some light on the "newness" of Bach's. If Bach is to escape the fate to which the philosopher of music, Theodor W. Adorno, feared he had already been condemned--that of "a composer for organ festivals in well-preserved Baroque towns"(28)--then we should probably recast him in Schoenberg's image, as Bach the Progressive.

T 5.1   Motivic Plan of Fuga VI in D Minor, WTC 1

Part 2   Part 1

Coda; on a
and Ia

Example, 5.1 (a)   J.S. Bach, <u>Fuga VI a 3, D Minor</u>, from <u>The Well-Tempered</u>
<u>Clavier</u>, Book-1.

Example, 5.1 (b)

Example, 5.2. Fuga VI, mm. 1-4

Example, 5.3. Fuga VI, reduction of mm. 3-4

Example, 5.4. Fuga VI, mm. 22-26, top voice

Example, 5.5. Fuga VI, corresponding cadential gestures,
mm. 18-20, 40-42

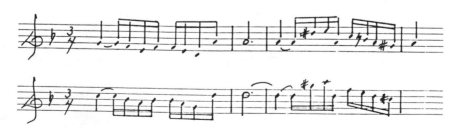

Small-case letters refer to the thematic fragments labelled in Table 5.1. Superscript numbers refer to diatonic transpositions upward. The process of transposition, especially in the case of tonal answers, must of course be interpreted somewhat freely. "I" indicates inversion, and "x" indicates material not obviously derived from the basic material - a, b, c, or d. The three voices have been labelled, from top to bottom, S, A/T (as the middle voice occupies both the alto and tenor range), and B. Linear statements of the basis melodic material appear under brackets. Corresponding areas in the parallel halves of the fugue are presented in boxes.

NOTES

1.   Arnold Schoenberg, "Bach," (1950), in Style and Idea: Selected Writings of Arnold Schoenberg, ed. Leonard Stein (New York: St. Martin's Press, 1975), p. 393. All further page number references to Schoenberg's essays are from Style and Idea, unless otherwise noted.

2.   Ibid., p. 397.

3.   See especially Walter Frisch, Brahms and the Principle of Developing Variation (Berkeley: University of California Press, 1984); and also Walter Frisch, "Brahms, Developing Variation, and the Schönberg Critical Tradition," 19th-Century Music 5 (1982); 215-32. Carl Dahlhaus has written extensively on the application of Schöenberg's principle to the music of the late nineteenth and early twentieth centuries. He presents his views concisely in Between Romanticism and Modernism, tr. Mary Whittall (Berkeley: University of California Press, 1980), pp. 45-52.

4.   Schöenberg, "Bach," p. 397, see also "Linear Counterpoint" (1931), p. 290.

5.   The two principles are directly contrasted in the following essays by Schöenberg: "On Revient Toujours" (1948), pp. 108-9; "New Music, Outmoded Music, Style and Idea" (1946), pp. 115-16; "Twelve-Tone Composition" (1923), p. 208; "National Music I" (1931), pp. 170-71; "Linear Counterpoint," p. 290; "Ornaments and Construction" (1923), p. 312; and "Bach," p. 397. See also his "Faschismus ist kein Exportartartikel" (1935), in Stil und Gedanke Aufsätze zur Musik, hrsg. Ivan Vojtech, Gesammelte Schriften I (Frankfurt: Fischer, 1976), p. 318; and his Fundamentals of Musical Composition, ed. Gerald Strang and Leonard Stein (London: Faber & Faber, 1967), p. 142.

6.   The point is made clearly in Schoenberg's "New Music, Outmoded Music, Style and Idea," p. 116, where he asserts that when composers have filled one direction of musical space with "content to the utmost capacity," they will do the same in the next direction, "and finally in all the directions in which music expands."

7.   See in particular Schoenberg's "On Revient Toujours," p. 109.

8.   See Schoenberg's discussion of the Minuetto from Mozart's String Quartet in A major, K. 464, where he claims that a "rare fusion" of the homophonic and contrapuntal styles occurs, in his Fundamentals of Musical Composition, p. 142.

9.   See Schoenberg's two essays: "Twelve-tone Composition," pp. 207 -8 and "National Music I," p. 171.

10. On the importance of contrapuntal combinations in primarily homophonic works (variations by Beethoven and Brahms), see Schoenberg, Fundamentals of Musical Composition, pp. 172-73. On the importance of the notion of developing variation in the works of a composer who was principally a contrapuntist (but who, according to Schoenberg, also initiated the technique of developiong variation), that is J. S. Bach, see Schoenberg's "National Music I" and "National Music II" (1931), pp. 171, 173; see also his Fundamentals of Musical Composition, p. 62.

11. Schoenberg's phrase "musical prose" is usually more narrowly defined as the tendency, in the music of the great German composers from the later eighteenth century onward, toward concision and brevity. As a result of its avoidance of formulaic padding, musical prose is character- ized by a syntax free from foursquare, periodic phrase construction. While Schoenberg did, at one point, appear to associate musical prose primarily with asymmetrical phrase construction (in "Brahms the Progres- sive," 1947, pp. 414-16, a consideration of this category within the broader framework of Schoenberg's aesthetic theory as a whole suggests that the fusion of the processes of development and unravelling is more fundamental to its definition. (See my earlier discussion of this point, pp. 51-3).

12. Schoenberg, "Bach," p. 397. Schoenberg gives a similar account of unravelling in "Linear Counterpoint," p. 289.

13. See also Schoenberg "On Revient Toujours," p. 109. In practice, however, the theme of a contrapuntal work is treated as a static entity only in works like the chorale prelude, where the basic melodic material is a preexistent tune. See also his "Folkloristic Symphonies" (1947), p. 165.

14. Schoenberg, "Faschismus," in his Stil und Gedanke, p. 318.

15. Schoenberg, "On Revient," p. 109.

16. On the combinative principle in general, see the following two essays by Schoenberg: "Fugue" (1936), p. 297 and "National Music II," p. 173. On the importance of invertible counterpoint, see his Fundamentals of Musical Composition, p. 85.

17. Schoenberg railed against the very idea of "linear counterpoint" in his essay of the same name, pp. 289-95.

18. Schoenberg, "Bach," p. 396.

19. Ibid.

20. Schoenberg discusses the role of developing variation in pri- marily contrapuntal works in his brief essay, "Fugue," p. 297. See also fn. 10.

21. Schoenberg; Style and Idea, p. 414. It was his purpose in writing "Brahms the Progressive" to show the extent to which Brahms moved in the direction of an "unrestricted musical language;" namely, to in- vestigate the nature of his musical prose. On Mozart and musical prose, see the same essay, pp. 411-16, 435-38. On Bach and musical prose, see Schoenberg's "New Music, Outmoded Music," pp. 117-18.

22. See Schoenberg; "Brahms the Progessive," pp. 409-11, 415-22, 435-38. Carl Dahlhaus sees Schoenberg's musical prose chiefly in terms

of phrase-length asymmetry. See especially "Musical prose and endless melody," in Dahlhaus; Between Romanticism and Modernism, pp. 52-54, where he links musical prose with Wagner's concept of "endless melody." Hermann Danuser, in his Musikalische Prosa, Studien zur Musikgeschichte des 19. Jahrhundets, Bd. 46 (Regensburg: Bosse, 1975), p. 132, defines Schoenberg's musical prose, perhaps too broadly, as the mediation of logical rational constructivism and apparent freedom.

23.   See the following two essays by Schoenberg: "A Self-Analysis" (1948), p. 78 and "My Evolution" (1949), pp. 80-81.

24.   Schoenberg; "New Music, Outmoded Music," p. 116.

25.   Schoenberg; "Brahms the Progessive," pp. 399-401.

26.   Berg implied the same in his essay "Why is Schönberg's music so hard to understand?" Music Review 13 (1952); 191-95 (trans. A. Swarowsky and J. J. Lederer; orig. publ. as "Warum is Schönbergs Musik so schwer verständlich?" in Musikblätter des Anbruch, 6, 1924). Schoenberg's music, according to Berg, presents great difficulties to the listener because of the "boundless opulence" of its musical prose. The "riches" of Schoenberg's language are primarily the result of his simultaneous combination of the polyphony of Bach and the thematic elaboration (developing variation) of the Viennese Classicists. In the same spirit, T. W. Adorno noted in his essay, "Arnold Schoenberg, 1874- 1951," in Prisms (trans. of Prismen, 1967, by Samuel and Sherry Weber, Cambridge, MA.: MIT Press, 1981), p. 149), that Schoenberg's music de- manded an "acute sensitivity to simultaneous multiplicity" from the listener.

27.   Schoenberg, Style and Idea, p. 118.

28.   T. W. Adorno, "Bach Defended against his Devotees," in Prisms, p. 136.

6

The Message of Johann Sebastian Bach in Ingmar Bergman's Cinematic Art

Fritz Sammern-Frankenegg

The following essay is based on a ninety minute multimedia lecture that I presented at Hofstra University as a preconference event on October 23, 1985. The five films that I had investigated for the expanded preconference lecture are Wild Strawberries (1957), Through a Glass Darkly (1961), The Silence (1963), Persona (1965), and Cries and Whispers (1972).

As a thematic point of reference, I chose to introduce my lecture with the opening of Bach's motet; "Fürchte dich nicht, ich bin bei dir" (Be not afraid, I am with you). I concluded with a musical quotation from the motet "Der Geist hilft unserer Schwachheit auf" (The Spirit helps us in our weakness) which summarizes what, in my understanding, seems to be the quintessence of Bach's message in the five Bergman films I investigated: the spirit's unifying, healing power in a world of anxiety and brokenness. Needless to say, Bergman has not made use of either these or other choral works by Bach, which would have allowed us to point out a message by means of words, a title, or a text line. Ingmar Bergman, master of the reduced form of chamber film, chose to let Bach have his say in wordless music mostly for single instruments-in a fugue from the Well-Tempered Clavier, in an excerpt from the Goldberg Variations, in sarabandes from Suites for Unaccompanied Cello, from a Partita for keyboard, and once in a violin concerto.

Bergman does not drown his audience in music. However sparsely and economically used in his mature films, music has a well-conceived artistic function and a strong emotional impact. In most of his mature films we find only little or no composed film music. Instead, Bergman selected excerpts from a great musical heritage, from George Frideric Handel, Domenico Scarlatti, Wolfgang Amadeus Mozart, Robert Schumann, and Frederic Chopin, to name a few, but above all from Johann Sebastian Bach. Among the nearly fifty films Bergman has made, no less than nine make artistic use of music by Bach.

For Wild Strawberries (1957), his first film with music of Bach, Bergman had film music composed by Erik Nordgren. Under his directorship, Nordgren made artistically effective use of one of Bach's most acclaimed fugues from the Well-Tempered Clavier, the Fugue in D- sharp Minor (Book 1, no. 8). Richard Wagner considered it the best of all the forty eight fugues, and Wilfrid Mellers, the British Bach scholar, counted it "among the wonders of European music."(1)

The "Bach scene" in Wild Strawberries belongs to a sequence of dream scenes in which Isak Borg, a successful scientist, and now an old man who is afraid of death, is being confronted with his past. When young, he lost his love, Sarah, to his brother Sigfrid. In a dream sequence in which Isak is presented as an old man and the remembered characters as they were at the time, he meets Sarah at the strawberry patch outside the family's summer house. She holds up a mirror for him and then runs to a baby carriage to comfort her sister's child. The film music starting at this point creates an uncanny atmosphere by means of chromatic scales and by a sequence of intervals that anticipates the beginning of the Bach fugue to be introduced shortly therafter. At a closer look, the two-interval sequence (E to B to C) used as the basic form of a threat motif, is identical with the two opening intervals of the fugue (B to F= sharp to G), a rising fifth and a half step.(2) The difference between the two comparable sequences is one of rhythm: The threat motif stresses the half step, and the fugue the rising fifth. The emotional equivalent to such musical difference is a contrast between threat and reassurance that becomes noticeable as the fugue, with its calm, long-breathed, bridge-like bows, replaces the anxious, chromatic advances of the threat motif. Careful attention makes us recognize that the threat motif coincides, as a counterpoint, with Sarah's comforting, reassuring words for the baby: "Don't be afraid, I am with you. I am holding you tight. Don't be afraid, little child. It will soon be day again. Nobody will hurt you. I am with you."

These reassuring words for an anxious infant which, in a secular setting, clearly strike a religious theme of Johann Sebastian Bach (quoted earlier from his motet "Be not afraid, I am with you"), anticipate the entrance of the fugue and its reassuring impact. There is, however, an important link of imagery to be considered as Bergman, after Sarah's departure, lets the old man step into a prepared setting of a symbolic image: the empty baby carriage on one side and another significant image on the other side, which is first hidden in the upper right corner of a long shot but then revealed in a close-up of two branches resembling a fork or the claws of a huge insect—an image of death. Clearly, such the sequence of shots (accompanied by the threat motif) of the young woman, comforting an infant child, and the old man's anxious appearance in the same image setting (symbolizing the human condition of being between birth and death), forms a symbolic reference structure that to me indicates the old man's need of comfort.

It is in such context of a cinematic structure with its integration of image, word, and sound that Bergman makes use of Bach's master fugue, which has been interpreted not only in musicological but also in theological terms. According to Wilfrid Mellers's twofold interpretation, which tries to do justice to Bach's combination of music and theology, the rising fifth, which is the opening interval of the fugue, has traditionally been understood as "a synonym for God."(3)   With such a knowledge of context, it is tempting to hear a religious message in Bergman's use of the fugue: Bergman starts the fugue only a few moments after he lets the old man's serious face in a quick close-up dissolve emerge from the embracing image of death, and right after another half-tone reference to the threat motif. Is the professor religious? The question is raised in an earlier scene by an agnostic student of science, representing the younger generation. The old scientist refuses an answer, but he has just recited a popular religious poem. Religion is not a central issue in Wild Strawberries, nor does it seem to be crucial in this Bach sequence which, in its further development, focuses on the issue of love, both fulfilled and lost. Bach's music, which magically attracts the old man, comes from the illuminated window of the house, but before he finds out that Sarah is playing the fugue for her future husband, Sigfrid, the camera shows him walk toward the light. This metaphor of light shining in the darkness contributes to the full meaning of the music in this scene.

By the time the old man has arrived at the house, in a close-up portrait against the shining window pane as he searches for the source of the music, the fugue's first five bars and the beginning of the sixth have been played. In order to return to the beginning of the fugue, which was needed for the structure of the following section, Bergman had his film composer write a one-bar transition. In my understanding, the following indoor scene of the Bach-sequence visualizes a basic feature of fugue technique. The dux--comes (leader-companion) structure of a fugue can suggest a love duet, and this is what Bergman seemed to have had in mind when he visually created (i.e., choreographed) the structure of a fugue in a musical arrangement of the couple's conduct and movements. As Sarah plays the theme-introducing leader voice (dux), Sigfrid, as her receiving companion, listens attentively and watches her, nodding slightly, and prepared to respond in a moment. His response coincides rhythmically with the music's response: He bows down to her and kisses her neck, as the comes (companion) voice starts with a rising fourth. In the economy of a short scene, Bergman uses the comes part not only for the male companion's response, but also for the following female's answer, namely, for both companions' mutual responses in love, as they look at each other and unite in a kiss. As the woman responds to her partner's caress, the performance of the fugue at the piano is interrupted. The piano, however, is replaced by the vibrating sound of a cello which repeats half a bar, accompanies the lovers' caressing and continues to the end of the scene. The fugue's comes-voice ends with both companions walking to the supper table. The rest of the music is not Bach's any longer, but Bergman's assisting composer uses the opening intervals of the fugue again, in a sequence of tones that reminds us of the earlier threat motif but has lost its threatening character, as the two companions join each other for a meal and raise their glasses. As in other Bergman films, eating and drinking together suggests a union: communion in love and companionship. The carefully composed indoor scene of this Bach sequence ends in a slow dissolve back to an image of isolation and threat: the old man staring into a cold night sky, an image that has been musically anticipated in a chromatic reference to the threat motif. The message of Bach in the cinematic structure of Wild Strawberries has the dimension of a religious message, reminiscent of the Old Testa- ment text that Bach has used in his motet "Fürchte dich nicht! Ich bin bei dir. Ich bin dein Gott." (Be not afraid! I am with you. I am your God.) It is, however, used in a secularized setting of love, projected into a dream vision by the old man's awakening sense of loss, and a judgment on his failure to recognize and treasure a deeper meaning of love in his youth.

The three films of A Film Trilogy (Through a Glass Darkly, 1961; Winterlight/The Communicants, 1962; and The Silence, 1963), which also has been called Bergman's "God trilogy," were intended to have a musical link in Bach's "Sarabande" from the Suite No. 2 for Unaccompanied Cello. However, Bergman gave up the idea because "it felt like a gimmick, something irrelevant, something contrived," as he admitted in a television interview. "Besides," the interviewer asked, "wasn't the effect rather sentimental?" "Yes," Bergman replied, "a romantization. Oddly enough, as that suite is very far from being sentimental."(4) This statement sheds some light on the artistic function of Bach's music in Bergman's films beyond the special occasion: It was not going to be misused as a mood-maker.

Bergman restricted the cello "Sarabande" to the first film, Through a Glass Darkly. For The Silence he chose the Goldberg Variations, Variation No. 25, and, as to The Communicants (Winterlight), he decided against using Bach, or rather music by Bach. He could not do without at least a hidden reference to the master by using the letters S.D.G. behind the dating of his film: Soli Deo gloria (To God alone the glory), Bach's distinctive theological trademark on many of his works.

In Through a Glass Darkly, the opening of the cello "Sarabande" from the Suite No. 2 is used no less than four times: In the title sequence, the music begins immediately after the opening bible quotations:

For now we see through a glass darkly, but then face to face
Now I know in part, then I shall know fully, even as I am
known.

Bergman leaves out the conclusion of this famous passage from Paul´s First
Letter to the Corinthians (chapter 13), which would certainly fit the
film´s issue:

So faith, hope and love abide; these three; but the greatest
of these is love.

With these well-known words being committed, it is the music of Bach that
carries the message. When repeated after Karin´s reading of her father´s
diary entry about the artist´s curiosity to register the allegedly hope-
less course of Karin´s illness, the music seems to serve as a counterpoint referring to the message of hope and love that the father has
betrayed.
    The music´s repetition in the shipwreck sequence occurs in reference
to the incestuous experience of brother and sister, as Karin, in an attack of her illness, had seduced Minus: Back in the house to pick up
blankets, Minus, in his despair as well as in his care for the his sick
sister, falls on his knees, silently praying (while we hear the foghorns´
uncanny sounds). The "Sarabande" sets in right after the brother speaks
a loud one-word prayer; "God!" on the same tone as the second foghorn.
The camera makes a jump cut from the praying brother´s face to the
couple, focusing first on the sick sister´s troubled face, then completing the composition in a slow pan to also include the brother. With the
music still playing, the camera now cuts to a long shot with a most
interesting image composition: The symbolic image of devastation gains a
transcendent dimension as we can, in the pattern of beams at the water-
filled bottom of the boat, clearly recognize the shape of a huge cross.
In the context of the story´s given situation, with the indicated interplay of word, image and music, it seems possible to see reflected here a
message of hope and love--superimposed against the despair of life.
    For an adequate understanding of the music´s function in the film´s
final sequence, it seems important to consider the following wider context of story and imagery: The film´s plot centers around Karin´s illness and how it affects all characters: David, (her father,) her brother
Minus, and her husband Martin, with whom she is vacationing on an island.
Toward the end of the film, after a devastating attack of her illness,
Karin wants to be sent back to the hospital. An ambulance helicopter
will pick her up. Shortly before its arrival, Karin disappears. They
find her in the empty attic, talking to the wall. Voices from another
world tell her that now will occur what had been promised to her earlier:
That the door in the wall will open and God will reveal himself. Martin
tries in vain to talk her out of her hallucination. He finally gives in
to her request to fall on his knees and together with her to await the
arrival of God. After a while, as the wall is vibrating during the heli-
copter´s arrival, the door opens. No god appears. Instead, in a terrifying hallucinatory experience triggered by the helicopter´s noise and the
probable appearance of its shadow on the wall, a spider comes through the
door and, according to her later description, crawls over her and tries
to rape her. In my undestanding, the imagery of this scene--that is,
both the repeated image of the father standing behind the open door and
the image of the descending helicopter, made visible through the window
behind Karin--has an important bearing on the Bach scene ahead.
    In this powerful scene of a schizophrenic´s hallucinatory experience
of faith and its terrifying disillusionment, Bergman seems to have more
in mind than merely a neurotic case. In accordance with Sigmund Freud´s
theory, his cinematic presentation of a neurotic experience seems to

serve the purpose of a psychoanalytic reduction of religion. The repeated image device of the sick woman's father at the open door in her sexually oriented religious experience is an unmistakable reference to Freud's psychoanalytic explanation of religion in which "the parental complex is understood as being the root of religious desire." ("Psychoanalysis has taught us the intimate connection between the father complex and a belief in God, has shown us that the personal god is psychologically nothing else than an elevated father.")(5)

The image of a descending helicopter can be seen as a symbolic reference in the visualized reduction process, in the destruction of a father god image that is taken down from its false heaven. In the film's final sequence, Bergman presents the image of a rising helicopter and combines it with the soaring, solemn sound of Bach's Sarabande--in the context of a cinematic structure that refers, in word, sound and image, to the development of a new concept of God. The discussion between father and son in the film's final scene, which is linked to the preceding helicopter scene by a short continuation of Bach's Sarabande, centers around the thought that love "as something real in the world of men proves God's existence or is itself God." David lets his "emptiness, his dirty hopelessness rest in that thought. Suddenly the emptiness turns into wealth, and hopelessness into life. It's like a pardon, Minus. From sentence of death."(6)

In my understanding, these words could be applied to the impact of Bach's music in the preceding scene sequence. It seems as if Bergman had coined them in reference to the sequence that begins with an image of emptiness and despair after Karin's departure (Minus in the big, empty hall) and suddenly changes to wealth, as Bergman lets the scared brother open the door and watch the rising helicopter. There is a perfect balance in this scene of music and images--the vibrating, solemn sound of Bach's Sarabande combined with alternating images of Karin's caring brother and the rising, soaring aircraft that will take the sick sister to the necessary hospital care. According to the film script, the aircraft is to be "swallowed up in the sunshine."(7) In the filmed scene, its disappearance in the sunlit evening sky is achieved by a slow dissolve to an image of sunset at the coast with a wide, infinite perspective of the glaring sea. This effective cinematic device helps to create the transcendent, spiritual quality of the scene. In the context of an ongoing thought process, the images of a descending and of a rising helicopter can be understood as symbolic images indicating two phases of a "reduction": The first image helps visualize the destruction of an obsolete, questionable god image. The second image, however, the ascending aircraft with the soaring sound of Bach's "Sarabande" refers to the rise of a new religious experience. The god concept at which the film's final scene arrives--that "God is love or love is God"--is to be found in the New Testament, in the Gospel of John, and within the Acts of the Apostles, in the First Letter of John:

> God is love. He who dwells in love, dwells in God and
> God in him.
>
> (1 John, 4:17)
> God himself dwells in us, if we love each other; his
> love is brought to perfection in us.
>
> (1 John, 4:12)

That Bergman in his next film, The Communicants (Winter Light) "unmasked" the "certainty achieved"(8) in Through a Glass Darkly and how he went about it does not concern us in this inquiry. Although he gave up the idea of using Bach's Sarabande from the second cello suite again, it is interesting that he seemed to have given thought to utilizing the music as a counterpoint to images of death and living death: "He will put it in during Marta´s and Tomas´ car drive (when we see their profiles through death´s floating tree shadows)."(9) "Now we are at the scene of the suicide. Now Gunnar Bjornstrand is walking back alone to the car: "and there, there Bach must come!" (I did not know that he was going to have Bach in this of all scenes.)(10)

The Silence (1963), the concluding film of the God trilogy, presents, according to Bergman´s comment, the "negative impression [print]" of "God´s silence,"(8) a world of hostility, with two sisters (Anna and Ester) who are not able to show each other tenderness, and a ten-year-old boy, Johan, who is caught between them, loving them both. The two sisters have been understood as representing body and mind. Bergman himself called Anna the body, and Ester the soul, and talked about "the tumult arising between body and soul when God is no longer there."(11)

During the production of The Silence, Bergman referred to the "reduction" reached in this film, and called it "a world utterly without God. In which only the hand--fellowship--is left. And the music."(11) As for the music, he not only chose Bach, he made the word BACH the center of a coded "secret message," consisting of six words, foreign words for Spirit, Anxiety, Joy, Face, Hand, and in the middle of them, the word Bach. I will return to this enigmatic secret message later. As to the meaning of Bach, Bergman avoided an explanation: "And Bach means Bach of course."(11)

To satisfy our curiosity, let us have a close look at the one scene in which Bach is played in this film. It seems important to pay attention to the context that Bergman created for this scene: After a confrontation between the sisters that mirrors their dichotomy of body and mind, Ester watches some older people follow the church bells call for service. We see her in an observer position at the window. She seems to reflect her spiritual situation in her exclusion from a security of faith, which is offered by the church. In the image setting of this scene, the reappearance of a horse-drawn carriage with old furniture could be understood as a symbolic reference to the homeless existence of those without the shelter of a faith. At this moment, when Ester seems to ponder her situation in a world without God, in the "silence of God"-- which was the film´s original title--she is touched by the soft, almost inaudible sound of harpsichord music.

Bergman took the music from one of Bach´s late, speculative masterpieces, the Goldberg Variations. He chose Variation no. 25, which alienates the "Aria" theme in a minor key and in a complex, strongly chromaticized and syncopated structure. Wilfrid Mellers calls it "passion music," "music as densely charged as the ´Arioso´ of the St. John´s Passion," and refers to Wanda Landowska, the legendary Bach interpreter on harpsichord, who named this variation "the crown of thorns."(12) The music is a perfect choice for the passion of the two symbolically presented sisters, who are separated and alienated, fighting each other in a hostile world without God.

The music comes through a radio, which Ester picks up before she sits down at the table. Let us have a close look at the composition of a remarkable shot. It is dominated by Ester sitting in the foreground listening to Bach, holding the radio, as if she received the message of his music through her hands and through the light shining on her face.

Hand and Face are the most important metaphors throughout this film, expressing their symbolic function within the secret six-word message of Ester´s letter to Johan. The hand, in a long radition of its understanding as a metaphor, has been called "the outside brain of man" by the German philosopher Immanuel Kant. Accordingly, the image of the hand can be used artistically as a symbolic reference to the spiritual act of receiving, grasping, and understanding. The compositional device of having the light shine on Ester´s face is in agreement with a well-known biblical metaphor of blessing, used in the benediction of Lutheran and

other Christian church services: "The Lord make his face shine upon you
and be gracious unto you. The Lord lift up his countenance upon you and
give you peace." Bergman´s nonverbal reference to the Lutheran benedic-
tion--the image of the light shining upon the face--ties in with Ester´s
remark in a suppressed note of the script about "a moment of peace"(13)
that she received in a listening to Bach. With such an observation, we
have touched on a visual reference to a religious, Christian dimension of
Bach´s message in this scene, which is remarkable in the context of
Ester´s earlier demonstrated alienation from a Christian church.

The foreground figure in this extraordinary shot--Ester listening
to Bach´s music and receiving its message--is framing, embracing as it
were, in a half-circle, the two figures in the background, Anna and
Johan, mother and son. In the symmetry of this beautiful visual composition, the couple is located between the accentuated images of Face and
Hand. The door between the two sisters is wide open in this film of
frequent door closing.

This intriguing shot would express harmony if it were not for words
to "Will Ester Come Along?" "I don´t know," indicate separation to come:
Bergman will in a moment cut to a close-up of mother and son, hugging in
a slightly rocking movement to the rhythm of the music. I find it most
significant that the boy, at this moment of harmony in a perfect balance
of music and imagery, asks for the name of a foreign city--"Timoka," a
name that Bergman took from the Estonian word for hangman, or execution-
er. A moment´s peace in a situation of human brokenness, comes in a
foreign city at war.

Anna´s way of expressing her love for the boy is not gentle to be
sure. Johan does not seem to feel comfortable with the somewhat aggres-
sive nature of his mothers sensuality. In contrast, the subsequent shot
of Ester listening to Bach radiates an aura of spirituality. Bergman has
illuminated not only the beauty of her face from above: Her left hand is
also carefully spotlighted from a different light source.

The kind old waiter enters the room and joins the three characters
for another remarkable composition. As Bergman has the waiter appear
with some sort of liquor for Ester, he makes him part of a most interesting and significant image arrangement: two couples--one in the foreground and one in the background--with the four of them listening to
Bach.

I had watched the development of the Bach scene several times before
I made a most surprising discovery about this shot: All of a sudden I
saw the structure of a cross. Take a good look at how Bergman, the experienced, ingenious director of theater and film, staged and arranged
this shot; take a three-dimensional look at this configuration of Bach-
listeners, include yourself--(it is after all your point of view, or
rather the film director´s point of view that you have gained)--and you
have the structure of a cross. Draw a horizontal line from the couple in
the foreground (from Ester to the old man), and a vertical line from the
viewer to the couple in the background, and you have a cross. In such a
cross configuration, or cruciform image, we are all united in listening
to a message in Bach´s music, we, the viewers, Bergman, whose pespective
we have gained, and the four characters he created.

Bergman´s cross image of Bach listeners, which we discovered here by
including ourselves, is not restricted to this shot. For its cinematic
unfolding in the development of moving pictures we have to see and consider the vertical line of Ester--Anna/Johan in a previous shot (discussed earlier), as well as the vertical line of Ester-Johan-Anna in a
subsequent shot. The cross form of this cinematic structure is not only
one of related visual images, united by music, but also of words. Words
are scarce in this scene, as well as in the whole film; the most important words are Johann Sebastian Bach. The naming of Bach occurs in both
directions of the cross structure, on its horizontal as well as on its

vertical line, in the laconic communication between Ester and the old man
as well as between Ester and her sister.

Bergman´s cross-shape naming of Bach reminds me that the name Bach
has been found to contain a cross structure in its German musical notation, with lines drawn between the B and the H (the German equivalent of
B-flat and B-natural) and between the A and the C. Bach made magnificent
musical use of his name in his later, highly speculative work, toward the
unfinished end of his Art of Fugue as well as in his Canonic Variations
on "Vom Himmel hoch, da komm ich her." As to a cross structure in Bach´s
works, scholars and teachers of Bach have pointed it out in the horizontal lines of melody and counterpoint and in the vertical lines of chords
of harmony or disharmony that Bach is known to have not avoided on his
way to harmonious conclusions.

In a closer look at the naming of Bach in both directions of
Bergman´s cinematic cross image, it is interesting to investigate the
somewhat strange fact that Ester leaves out Bach´s first name (Johann) in
both references. The old waiter, after repeating the unusual abbrevi-
ation, completes the name--Sebastian Bach. Johann Sebastian Bach. In
the second reference, Johann is left out again but is not filled in
retrospectively. What happened to Johann? Why play such a game with
Bach´s familiar first of two Christian names? There is a way of calling
attention to something important by leaving it out. Thus, the word to
attract our particular attention is Johann.

When the old waiter reinserts the name, he gives it an unusual
accent, stressing on the second syllable: Jo hann´. Such an accent
might be taken as allegedly characteristic of the foreign language
(which, however, is invented), but I have a hunch that there is more to
it. The unusual accent Jo hann´ reminds me of the name´s full biblical
form, Johannes which is used in both German and Swedish, not only in
traditional name giving (as in Johannes Brahms), but more important--for
our context--for the name John in the New Testament, for both the John of
the Gospels and the John of the Act of the Apostles (Johannes-Evangelium
and Apostel Johannes). Jo´hann becomes Johann and then Johannes. If we
take this word game, with the omission of Johann and the name inserted as
Johann, seriously--and I suggest we should--we discover a most interesting and important theological reference in the center of the cruciform
image of this Bach scene. (Such a device would be in accordance with the
fact that Bach´s own musical cross structure had theological implications.) Consider the possibility of a hidden reference in Bergman´s
cruciform image to the gospel of John, the letters of John the Apostle or
both.

Recall the words of the Gospel (13:34): "I give you a new command-
ment: love one another, as I have loved you" and the words in the First
Letter of John from the Act of the Apostles: "Do not think that I am
giving you a new command; I am recalling the one we have before us from
the beginning: Let us love one another" (2 John 5).

The hidden reference to Johannes, the most spiritual among the four
evangelists reminds me of what Bergman, the son of a prominent Lutheran
minister must have known: that Nathan Söderblom, the renowned Swedish
archbishop, recommended Johann Sebastian Bach as the "fifth evangelist"
to the participants of the 1929 Ecumenical World Conference in Uppsala.

What about the hide-and-seek game with Johann on the vertical line
of Bergman´s Bach cross, namely: on the Ester-Johan-Anna line that
Bergman develops toward the conclusion of his sophisticated Bach scene?
I would like to draw your attention to its very subtle structure: Notice
Johan´s role as a mediator, as he picks up cigarettes that Anna had
requested from her sister. Pay attention to Bergman´s staging device of
letting the boy sit down at the door frame, the threshold between the two
divided sisters. I find it a most significant visual device that
Bergman, during this unusual communication between the sisters through an

open door, has Johan turn his head to each speaker, as if to emphasize
the importance of each word. He turns to the mother, as she wants to
know what music they are listening to, and then to Ester, after she has
said "Bach," in other words exactly during the short pause between the
last name and its incomplete expansion to Sebastian Bach. Thus, the
missing name Johann, with a visual reference to Johan the boy, is inserted silently into the empty spot. The short sequence now reads:

> Anna: "What music is that?"
> Ester: "Bach. ----- (pause, with Johan n s face turning to
>   Ester) Sebastian Bach."

The word game in this segment with the silent image of Johan the boy
replacing the word Johann, points in the same direction as the game in
the first segment, only in a more concrete way. Its symbolic understanding must not be separated from that of the previous one. In my understanding, it is another hidden reference to the unifying spirit of love.
Consider this: Throughout the film, from its very first scene, Johan is
placed in between the two alienated sisters who, in their symbolic representation of "body and mind"/"body and soul", belong together, yet do not
find each other in the films given situation of "God´s silence" ("a world
utterly without God.") Although moving closer to Ester (the intellect,
and the translator/interpreter) with his interest for the meaning of
words, and finally receiving her testament, in the form of a secret
message, he does not really take sides in the antagonism between the sisters. He loves them both and yearns to see them united. Thus, the boy
Johan represents a unifying tie in a broken relationship. Considering
such a constellation in the film´s structure, a hidden reference to the
gospel of love that I recognize in this Bach scene makes good sense.
Such a reference, however hidden and subtle as it is in the structure of
this scene, occurs in a kind of "negative print": in a cruciform image
of Bach listeners, listening to a variation that refers to its basic
theme, but only in the alienated, frequently modulated, chromaticized,
and syncopated form of a sarabande, in a wordless passion music with the
brittle sound of a harpsichord instead of the vibrating sound of a cello.
I have wondered about Ester´s "secret message" to Johan, which
Bergman secretively refuses to formulate but only indicates in a hidden
code of foreign words. I found good reasons, in the script as well as in
the film´s strategy, to identify the words as Spirit, Anxiety, Fear, Joy,
Bach, Face, Hand. I suggest that Ester, who toward the end of the film
will hand over a "letter" to Johan, receives the inspiration for her
secret message in the extraordinary spiritual experience of listening to
Bach that this unique scene demonstrates--an experience of peace and
harmony in a broken world. In the film script, Bergman has her refer to
that experience in a note in which the word BACH is united with the first
three words of the secret message:

> HADJEK = spirit, MAGROV = anxiety, fear, KRASGT - joy
> After these she had written: "We listened to BACH.
> A moment of peace. I felt no fear of dying."(13)

In the film´s final scene we see Johan read Ester´s letter, her testament. However, we cannot read the letter. In the final shot we see his
lips silently form the foreign words for Spirit and Anxiety. Before he
can even lip-read the third one, a strange word for Joy, the film ends.
Joy is beyond the world presented in this film, but it is a word in the
secret message....and seems to be the film´s secret message--a message of
Joy to be experienced in the unifying power of the Spirit, in a reunification of broken, separated, and alienated parts. Such a message seems
to be implied in the cruciform image of Ingmar Bergman´s most important

Bach scene, on both the horizontal and vertical line of a listening to
Bach: The message of Bach´s music, its unifying spiritual power, achieves
communication and communion across the dividing barriers of language and
across the dividing barricades of alienated sisters in "the silence of
God."

In a probable listing order of the six words, Joy is in the center,
together with Bach, the following word Bach is not a word in a foreign
language as are the rest yet it still must be discovered and understood
in its full importance.

Johan´s reappearance before and within the title sequence of Persona
(1965), with unmistakable references to Hand and Face, the central images
in The Silence, makes it clear that Bergman, through the boy´s perspective, is still involved in an ongoing understanding process concerning
Ester´s secret message. Closely connected with the imagery of Face and
Hand is again the music of Bach: Elisabeth, the actress who turned
silent during a performance of Sophocles´ Electra, listens to Bach in the
psychiatric clinic. The context is again important: Through the radio,
Elisabeth hears references to forgiveness and mercy that she finds hard
to accept. She becomes upset as she repeatedly hears, "Do you know what
mercy is?" The nurse switches programs. What words fail to accomplish,
asking for and accepting mercy, is achieved through a message in Bach´s
music. It is not the "Kyrie" in the Mass in B Minor to which we listen
with the mute actress, but rather the wordless "Adagio", the slow movement from the Violin Concerto in E Major. As we hear the music, we watch
close-ups of Elisabeth´s face and hand. First, we see her face from
above, with a glimmer of light on the forehead reminding me of the biblical metaphor used in The Silence. With the light diminishing, the face
turns slowly to a profile view, landscape-like as if to suggest the face
of humanity. Then, slowly, a hand approaches and finally covers the
face´s troubled contours. I would like to point out a wider context for
Elisabeth´s affliction: human atrocities committed not only in a drama
of antiquity, in Electra, but also in our century. The film includes
references to the war in Vietnam as well as to the ghetto of Warsaw.
This is listening to Bach in the twentieth century.

There is a clear link between this scene in Persona (1965) and one
of two Bach scenes in Cries and Whispers (1972). The link is in the
theme of forgiveness, which runs through Bergman´s films, and in the
symbolic imagery of Face and Hand, which are presented in close-up shots.
The importance of the secret message for Cries and Whispers, which was
made ten years after The Silence, is noticeable in the dominant imagery
of Face and Hand. It has been called "a symphony of hands"(14), and it
seems to me as that Bergman may have made the two Bach scenes in this
masterpiece of cinematic art with the six-word message from The Silence
in mind.

As to Bach´s music in Cries and Whispers, it is again the solemn, if
not sacral, dance form of a sarabande, this time from the Suite No. 5 for
Unaccompanied Cello. Not only does Bergman use the same "Sarabande" for
both scenes, he divides it in two sections, a longer and a shorter one,
which overlap. The longer section used for the first scene consists of
the first fifteen to twenty bars altogether; the shorter one consists of
the last eight bars. I will later come back to this interesting
structure, which seems to indicate the spiritual unity of both scenes.

Wilfrid Mellers characterizes this "Sarabande", which is entirely
monodic, as "harmonically powerful, even anguished, because its wide-
spread arpeggios frequently involve dissonant intervals. . . . The pain-
fully spread melody . . . remotely resembles--especially since the leaps
become . . . vast--Schoenbergian atonality." With a resemblance to
Schöenbergian atonality, this music forebodes Twentieth century musical
structure. Mellers continues with the observation of a paradox:
"paradoxically, however, the movement remains calm, almost disembodied:

physical (harmonic) anguish dissolves in meta-physical (melodic) grace. The music is a purgation."(15)

Bergman considered such wonderfully spiritual, "almost disembodied" music, which according to Mellers's observation, dissolves anguish in lgrace, to be appropriate to fit two centerpieces of his film. These are two scenes that both deal with a transformation of anguish into the grace of joy, first in a crucial encounter of two sisters, and then in a most powerful scene demonstrating a victory of fearless love over the horror of death.

As to the context of the story: Two sisters, Karin and Maria, have come home to their family's estate to be present at their sister Agnes's death from cancer. On the day of the funeral, Maria approaches Karin with the request that, during this trying time, they make an effort to come closer and to open themselves to each other. "Dearest Karin," she says, "couldn't we use these days we're together in getting to know one another, in getting close to one another. I can't stand distance and silence."(16) Distance and silence: This is a central theme of Bergman's, emphasized above all in The Silence. The two sisters, Karin and Maria, resemble Ester and Anna in a way that reminds me of the earlier symbolic pattern of mind and body: Karin is more intellectual, and Maria more sensual. Their attempts to come closer to one another are artistically presented in a sequence of dream-like scenes with close-ups of their hands and faces against a red background. After frustrating efforts to communicate, the sisters finally experience the grace of joy and peace in a loving encounter that momentarily tears down the walls of hatred, suspicion, guilt, and anxiety. When Karin asks Maria's forgiveness and they finally look at each other after repeated requests, anxiety miraculously turns into joy. The music breaks in to express the sudden transformation. (Its effect reminds me again of David's words in the final scene of Through a Glass Darkly: "Suddenly the emptiness turns into wealth and hopelessness into life. It's like a pardon. From sentence of death.")(6) Bergman's use of Bach's "Sarabande" surprisingly fits the scholar's interpretation that "anguish dissolves in grace." (15) A delicate sequence of close-ups shows the sisters' faces and hands from different angles during their ecstatic communion. As they speak to each other, their lips move but no words can be heard. The words belong to a foreign language, which is apparent in the joyful expression of their faces as they look at each other, in the tender touches of their caressing hands, and in the grace of Bach's music on the single cello. Thus, the six words hidden in Esters secret message (Spirit / Anxiety, Fear / Joy / Bach / Face / Hand) are all present in a sequence that starts out in a state of anxiety and fear and ends in the joy of peace.

The second Bach scene in Cries and Whispers concludes a dream sequence in which the two sisters are summoned to the deathbed of the deceased sister by Anna, her faithful and loving maid who had stayed with the dying woman and helped her through pain and anxiety by her loving presence. The whole sequence is acted out in the imagination of Anna, the maid. It deals with the problem of communication between the living and the dead shortly after the moment of death. Bergman pondered the problem and its possible artistic presentation in reflections between scenes of his printed story and said that he did not want to create a ghost scene.(17)

In the unusual, dream-like presentation of his mystic experience that a deceased person is longing for love in the void of death, which he called "the extreme of loneliness," he lets Agnes, on the night of her death, express her anxiety in an experience of total emptiness and in her wish that her sisters be close to her, hold her hands, warm her, and stay with her until the horror of death has passed. In Anna's dream sequence the living sisters are summoned to the deathbed and shown to be horrified at the dead sister's request.

The sisters' inability to cope with the horror of death is contrasted with Anna's fearless love for her dead mistress and friend: "Don't be
afraid. I'll look after her," and again in her words; "I stay with her."
With these words--"I stay with her"--Bergman has touched on a topic
treated by Johann Sebastian Bach. Bergman knows it and quotes him at
this point, although not in the famous motet that I quoted in my introduction   ("Be not afraid. I am with you.") Bergman avoids words; he
choses the wordless Sarabande which "dissolves anguish in grace."
     Note the significant visual composition at the introduction of this
Bach scene: As Anna has disappeared and joined Agnes in the chamber of
death, she has left behind her a world of anxiety that is visualized in
the following close-ups of the horrified sisters. Bergman presents them
in images of living dead, as if to counter and mock their earlier argument in favor of life (when summoned to her sister's deathbed, Karin had
said; "I am alive and I want nothing to do with your death"). In this
Bach scene Bergman has divided the music in half. The first four of the
eight bars he has assigned to images of living dead, as a significant
counterpoint. The second four bars (the last four bars of the "Sarabande") he has assigned to the image of Anna holding and cradling her
dead friend. In this Pieta section of the Bach scene, image and music
are in a balance of harmony. Anguish is dissolved in grace.
     I mentioned earlier that the two Bach scenes in Cries and Whispers
are linked by the same music, and, more specifically, by the fact that
this music, the "Sarabande" from the Cello Suite No. 5, is divided
between them in two over lapping parts. Such a structured musical link
seems to indicate a semantic link between the two scenes. There is
indeed a spiritual link between them, if we think about it: Both scenes
demonstrate the change of anguish and anxiety in distance and isolation
to a fearless communion of fellowship and love in a state of grace. The
earlier scene presents a communion of alienated sisters in a graceful
situation of life, and the later one a communion between maid and mistress which in fearless love bridges the horrifying gap of death. Thus,
both scenes illustrate, if only in images from dream sequences, a reunification of alienated, separated, isolates spheres in a spirit of
love: of sisters, of social classes, of life and death. I find it most
significant that such artistic visions of a reunification in the spirit
of love are created and emphasized with music by Johann Sebastian Bach.
The message of Bach's music in Ingmar Bergman's cinematic art is one of
the Spirit and of its unifying, healing power.
     Bach's music is an experience of the Spirit, moving us over the span
of centuries, acknowledging our Anxiety, our anguish in isolation, yet
changing it into graceful moments of Joy, in rhythm, melody, harmony,
fellowship, and love, extending beyond all borders and dividing barriers
in a world of hostility, catastrophe and brokenness.
     Finally, I would like to recall again Bergman's impressive image
from The Silence: of people divided by barriers, listening to Bach's
message. However, for the purpose of conclusion and summary only, I
would like to change the music. I would like to play the opening of a
motet that seems to carry Bach's basic message in its music as well as in
its text: "Der Geist hilft unserer Schwachheit auf" (The Spirit helps us
in our Weakness).

NOTES

     I wish to acknowledge the generous help of Gloria Eleana Bosque in
the correction of my manuscript.
     The multimedia lecture on which this article is based was only the
beginning of an ambitious project which would present my investigation
into Bergman's artistic use of Bach's music in the medium of film. While

the lectures restricted themselves to only five films and a limited presentation of projected film excerpts, the video programs make a more
satisfying use of the film's own artistic medium and deal with all ten
films in which Bergman plays or refers to music of Bach. In this article
I had to reduce the presentation of my analyses to merely verbal descriptions which cannot do full justice to the film's visual imagery. In the
video programs I have remedied such a deficiency. These are now available for purchase or rental at the University of California Extension
Media Center, 2176 Shattuck Avenue, Berkeley, Ca., 94704: The Message of
Johann Sebastian Bach in Ingmar Bergman's Cinematic Art. Video Series in
Five Parts, US Davis Instructional Media, 1988-89, Catalog § 37881-37885.

1. Wilfrid Mellers, Bach and the Dance of God, (New York: Oxford
    University Press, 1981), p. 46.

2. As it turns out, these intervals form the nucleus of the entire
    film's leitmotif, first presented in title sequence.

3. Wilfrid Mellers, Bach and the Dance of God, p. 39.

4. TV interview, February 7, 1963, recorded in Vilgot Sjöman, L 136.
    Diary with Ingmar Bergman, trans. Alan Blair (Ann Arbor: Karoma
    Publishers, 1978), p. 205.

5. Sigmund Freud, Leonardo da Vinci and a Memory of His Childhood
    (1910), Standard Edition of the Complete Psychological Works,
    vol. 9 (London: Hogarth Press, 1957), p. 123.

6. Ingmar Bergman, Three Films, tr. Paul Britten Austin (New York:
    Grove Press, Evergreen ed.) p. 61.

7. Ibid., p. 59.

8. Bergman's explanatory introduction to his Filmtrilogy reads: The
    theme of these three films is a "reduction"-in the metaphysical
    sense of that word.
    Through a Glass Darkly - certainty achieved.
    Winter Light - certainty unmasked.
    The Silence - God's silence-the negative impression.
    Ingmar Bergman, Three Films, trans. Paul Britten Austin, p. 7.

9. Vilgot Sjöman, L 136. Diary with Ingmar Bergman, p. 205.

10. Ibid., p. 219.

11. Vilgot Sjöman, L. 136. Diary with Ingmar Bergman, p. 222.

12. Wilfred Mellers, Bach and the Dance of God, p. 282.

13. Ingmar Bergman, Three Films, p. 131.

14. Tom Milne, Ingmar Bergman's Cries and Whispers, Monthly Film
     Bulletin 40 (March 1973), p. 61.

15. Wilfrid Mellers, Bach and the Dance of God, p. 34.

16. Ingmar Bergman, Four Stories, trans. Alan Blair (Garden City,
     New York: Anchor Books, 1977), p. 81.

17. Ibid., p. 86.

7

Bach's *Musical Offering* as Autobiography

Stephen A. Gottlieb

The story of the origin and composition of the <u>Musical Offering</u> (Musicalisches Opfer) appears in several sources. Bach´s famous meeting with King Frederick of Prussia occurred on May 7, 1747. we have a report in the Berlin newspaper, the <u>Spenersche Zeitung,</u> on May 11.(1)   A fuller account appears in Johann <u>Nikolaus Forkel´s</u> early biography (1802) of Bach and is based on an eyewitness report by Bach´s son, Wilhelm Friedemann.(2)   The story is that, at the start of one of King Frederick´s evening concerts, just as the king himself raised his flute to his lips, old Bach arrived at his son´s lodgings and immediately was summoned to the king. The king conducted Bach from room to room so that Bach could try out the new Silbermann <u>fortepianos.</u> After a while, Bach asked the king for a subject for a <u>fugal</u> improvisation. Frederick obliged, but also "commanded" a six-part fugue.

This story has several parts that are analogous to the composition and the form of the <u>Musical Offering.</u> To enumerate: First, there is the contrast between the <u>work´s</u> initial improvisation of the king´s theme (the three-part fugue) and the final six-part fugue that appears in the second <u>ricercare</u> of the finished work itself. Second, there is Bach´s substitution of his own theme, which was better suited for extemporaneous treatment than the king´s theme. At the original occasion, Bach did proceed to develop this substituted theme with six <u>obligato</u> parts. Third, there is the formal dedication of the <u>Musical Offering,</u> carefully worded and preceding the score itself. Here is embedded the story of Bach´s apology for not using the king´s theme for the extemporaneous six-part fugue. However, Bach´s humility is comical to the point of suggesting something more than beyond his formal respect. Bach wrote: "To obey Your Majesty´s command was my humble duty. I noticed very soon, however, that, for lack of necessary preparation, the execution of the task did not fare as well as the excellent theme demanded. This resolve has now been carried out as well as possible."(3) Bach´s apology is at once genuine and mock, as the inscription on the page preceding the first musical section demonstrates. It reads:

<u>Regis Iussu Cantio Et Reliqua Canonica Arte Resoluta.</u>

The inscription translates, "By the King´s Command, the Theme and the Remainder Resolved with Canonic Art."

Bach´s pun on the word <u>canonic</u> has been noticed by many commentators, including a recent one, <u>Douglas R. Hofsadter,</u> who noted that the word means both "with canons" and "in the best possible way."(4) Canonic art also means "proper art" or "with strict formality," emphasizing again the distinction between spontaneity and studied composition. The triple pun replays, with studied verbal art, the final statement of Bach's formal apology, but with humor, as though to say, "I've done the best I can" and well as "I've resolved the matter perfectly." The contrast between formlessness and form, resolution and lack of resolution, playfulness and seriousness, and more, appears in the story as well as in the resolution of the event in words and in the music that Bach would subsequently compose. The Musical Offering is an intricate and poignant instance of musical autobiography.

The oddities of this story are repeated in the oddities of the finished musical work. Some of the work's features seem, initially, to be mistakes. This is not so. Just as Bach fumbled, or so it seems, with King Frederick, so parts of the Musical Offering seem to be relatively fumbling efforts, at least for Bach. Here, however, we have a musical joke of the highest order, as well as, I will claim, Bach's autobiographical replication in music.

One interesting interpretation of the work is by Douglas Hofstadter. Although his approach depends on Hans Theodore David's analysis, Hofstadter provides the insight of a resourceful mathematician. King Frederick had given Bach a theme that, Hofstadter points out, "is a very complex one, rhythmically irregular and highly chromatic (that is, filled with tones which do not belong to the key it is in)."(5)   The challenge to compose any fugue on such a theme is a hard one, and Bach was commanded to create a six-part fugue. As Hofstadter points out, there are no six-part fugues in the forty-eight Preludes and Fugues of the Well-Tempered Clavier itself.(6)

Bach's response to the king's command provides, once again, a musico-autographical account. The inscription to the king (discussed above) is an acrostic that spells ricercare, a term that in Bach's time designated "an erudite kind of fugue."(7)   The word literally means a seeking out, thus suggesting the composition of a piece whose significance lies beyond itself.   The word fugue means a flight. The Musical Offering is, therefore, metaphoric, and its unity as well as its parts have metaphoric meaning as well as musical unity. The unity of the work cannot be assessed (although it may be appreciated), without an understanding of its etiology. The acrostic of the dedication, for instance, would seem to term the entire work a ricercare, although there are two ricercares, a trio sonata, and ten canons in the work.(8)   An application of the acrostic suggests that the mystery of the work is to be understood by studying the whole and its parts in relation to the king's command; and the essence of the command has to do with the most difficult fugue that can be imagined.   In the Musical Offering, Bach is stretching the form of music to signify many kinds of meaning.

The unity of the whole Musical Offering turns on its repeated use of puzzles. For instance, although the ten canons in the work are quite complex, none of them is fully written out. They therefore fall into the ricercare pattern of seeking solutions to mysteries. In fact, one of the canons (Canon a 2, a canon in contrary motion) is labelled "Quaerendo invenietis" ("By seeking, you will discover"). These canons also fall into the pattern whereby the part implies the whole, a pattern that Hofstadter sees as infinite looping.   Three of the canons are puzzle canons, whose notation is partially written out.   The crab canon's solution is suggested by an inverted clef at one end of the staff. Again we find a part that suggests the whole. This imagery of the whole and the part is replayed within each canon because, as Hofstadter notes, each canonic voice "copies" the theme, except where a voice has the sheer function of harmony, and is therefore a "free" voice.(9)   As indicated by the formal term ricercare, one must, in the canons, search for the theme. Consequently, we have an important interplay between restriction and freedom, form and content, and perhaps even between King Frederick and Bach the musician.

These oppositions compliment King Frederick by playfully turning the strictness of his command into strict musical form. That Bach recognized the musical metaphor may be seen in the canon per tonos, a three-voiced canon. Hofstadter's analysis of this canon, following David's, suggests the complexity in the metaphoric dimension of Bach's music. The king's theme is the upper voice. The lower voices are free harmonizations of another theme, a device that hints at Bach's substitution of his own theme during the original improvisation before the king. If one played the canon once, it would end in the wrong key; but if one played it six times, modulating upward from the original key of the lower voice (C minor), one would restore the original key. The successive modulations suggest the freedom of fantasia, yet the solution to the musical puzzle is achieved through a quite strict use of form, for the success of the trick depends on the middle voice being separated from the lower voice by a fifth. When the canon is finished, each voice ends one octave higher than it began, a "loop" that, in Hofstadter's analysis, suggests infinity.(10)   Bach wrote in the margin by this canon, "Ascendenteque Modulatione ascendat Gloria Regis" ("And as the modulation rises, so may the King's glory"). The structure, then, of the Musical Offering replicates the origins of its composition: Bach's original "fumbling" with the king's theme, his improvisation of a substitute theme, and the perfect fulfillment of the king's command in the Musical Offering itself. The choice of a set of variations, along with the uniform use of C minor and polyphonic structure form the basis of the work's coherence. Three forms are used, however, each with its symbolic implications. The ten canons and two ricercares are archaic forms, while the sonata (the centerpiece of the Musical Offering) was considered a more progressive style. The presence of the sonata at the work's center is a tribute to Frederick and to his flute. It may even be that Bach was satirizing Frederick's fashionable orchestra. Christoph Wolff noted that "the third movement of the sonata stresses . . . the reference to [the] characteristic style of the Berlin school in the 1740s and 1750s." The stylistic elements of the Empfindsamkeit sentimentality are used in the sonata's "extensive and lengthy interludes."(11)

As shown in Figure 7.1, the Musical Offering is organized according to a five-part symmetry:(12)

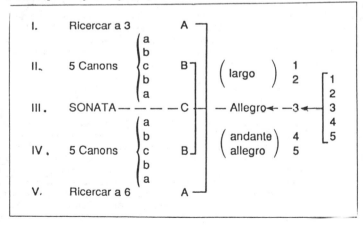

The trio sonata and the two ricercares possess a similar pattern, but the pattern is perfected only in the sonata and in the six-part ricercare. It is the interrelationships of these three sections that I will emphasize.(13)

The three-part ricercare, like the sonata and the six-part ricercare, uses the thema reguim as its subject. However, in the first ricercare the fantasia section sounds so different from its musical context in tonal quality that it stands out emotionally and structurally as an intentional error. According to David, such fantasia sections are formally acceptable when they appear at the exact center of a piece. Here, however, it appears within the recapitulation section, and consequently is off-center. As a result, the three-part ricercare conveys the impression of an improvised piece rather than "a fully worked-out and finished composition."(14) As Wolff points out, citing Johann Walther's Musicalisches Lexicon (Leipzig, 1732), there were two legitimate types of ricercare: the improvisational and the studied.(15) My argument is that Bach's three-part ricercare is a studied improvisation despite its apparent unreflective qualities. The imbalance is ingenious musically and carries autobiographical implications. As David realized, this first ricercare represents, and may even be, the original Postsdam fugue.

The trio sonata, moreover, addresses the problem of balance encountered in the first ricercare. Whereas both pieces develop "a contrasting section in which thematic elements are elaborated, opening and ending with clear-cut imitative treatment of these elements,"(16) the sonata positions the strongly contrasting section in its exact center. The way Bach achieved this symmetry is interestingly conspicuous and simple. Although the contrasting material appears in the second of the four movements, the second movement stands at the center of the sonata due to the extended length of the first movement, the Largo. Moreover, the contrasting material in this first of two allegros appears in the third of this movement's five sections, and even in the center of the third section.(17)

However, it is the final section of the Musical Offering, the six-part ricercare, that represents the fulfillment of the king's command because the problem of symmetry first introduced in the three-part ricercare needed to be solved in a six-part fugue. Corresponding sections of the two ricercari are similarly developed, but only to a certain extent. The proportions of the second ricercare are much more exact and balanced. In this work there are twelve entrances of the theme, six in the exposition and six throughout the remainder. As David said, "Secondary expositions are distributed through the entire form" so that there is no "contrasting middle section" (unlike the three-part ricercare or the trio sonata), and the balance is perfect. David concludes, "Thus the larger movements in the Musical Offering are, in certain respects, tied up with Bach's original improvisation."(18)   In addition, the interlocking structure of all the sections, including the canons, replicates the intellectual nature of the canon enigmaticus, or puzzle canon form. Furthermore, just as most of the canons in this work "can be repeated at will" (19) because they return to the form of their beginnings, so the ending of the Musical Offering solves the puzzling imperfection of its beginning. The Musical Offering, therefore, completes a circle and, simultaneously, imitates the "infinite" form of many of its parts.

However, not all commentators have agreed that the Musical Offering is a unified work. In 1880, Philip Spitta said, "As the whole collection now exists it is a strange conglomerate of pieces, lacking not only internal connection but external uniformity. . . In this work Bach renounced the introduction of any comprehensive idea which would unify the separate artistic creations."(20) Despite the odd layout of the original manuscript printings, however, most critics have proposed one or another overall plan for the work.

Christoph Wolff, who surveyed the troublesome manuscript problems that have prompted the fascinating debates on the work's structure,(21) notes that a complete "ordering principle is not unusual in Bach and occurs in the Goldberg Variations and in the Dritter Theil der Clavier übung bestehend in verschiedenen Vorspielen über die Catechismus--und andere Gesaenge, vor die Orgel. Works of "planned coherence" abound, although Wolff holds that only the Goldberg Variations "require a cyclical performance."(22)   Of the Musical Offering manuscripts, Wolff claims that "there is no hint whatsoever at any intended order for a complete cyclical performance," although he does suggest his preferred sequence.(23) Wolff accepts David's ordering of the larger pieces of the Musical Offering, but says of the canons: "Indeed the little pieces run through the entire work like a red thread or like an ingenious ornamentation of the print."(24) After surveying the disposition of the canons with regard to the manuscript history, Wolff concludes, "If Bach had wanted them and the grand pieces in a specific order he would have used any opportunity for making his desires clear."(25)

Ursula Kirkendale, however, accepts Wolff's ordering of the pieces but finds inner coherence in the ordering.(26)   Unlike Wolff, but like David, Kirkendale champions a cyclic order hypothesis. The case for a cyclic structure turns on one's sense of the precise conceptual design of the work's inner structure. That is, for Kirkendale and Wolff, a diplomatic study of the available manuscripts does not, as a sole method of inquiry, offer a solution to the ordering principle of the whole work.(27)

For Kirkendale, the ordering principle is Marcus Fabius Quintilian's Institutio Oratoria. Her thesis is that the sections of the Musical Offering "are functionally analogous to the parts of an oration" and that the work is therefore cyclic; provided, of course, that the parts are played in the correct rhetorical sequence.(28)   However, critics do not agree on the ordering of the parts, and we are drawn to postulate a multiple structure for the Musical Offering. Certainly, in the light of Kirkendale's strong argument, the Musical Offering may be seen to display a rhetorical basis beyond the ordinary persuasive force of "abstract" instrumental music. Kirkendale quotes Johann Nickolaus Forkel's statements: "Under his hand every piece spoke like an orator; Bach "regarded music as a language, the composer as a poet."(29) Then, also, Bach had taught Latin at St. Thomas in Leipzig. His rector at the Thomasschule had edited Quintilian's work.   Johan Abraham Birnbaum, a rhetorician at Leipzig University, had written of Bach, "He has such perfect knowledge of the parts and merits which the working out of a musical piece has in common with rhetoric."(30)

As an example of Kirkendale's method, let us consider the two canons, Canon a 2 and Canon a 4, which appear following the six-part ricercare in the original 1747 edition. The first of these, which is probably the second by implication of Kirkendale's reasoning, is preceded by Bach's remark, "quaerendo invenietis" ("By seeking you will find"). Kirkendale states that these canons appear where the argumentio section of the oration would appear. However, in rhetorical terminology, the argumentio was termed quaestiones.   In addition, "the argumentio was always divided into two parts, the probatio and the refutatio. In his discussion of the probatio, moreover, Quintilian had said, "I urge that one search ("ad Quaerendum"),   and I bear witness that discoveries ("inveniri") can be made".(31)

As Wolff noted, Bach would have been aware of the Biblical "Quaerendo invenietis" of Matthew 7:7. This allusion reinforces the reading of the Musicalisches Opfer title as "Musical Sacrifice."(32) In addition, Kirkendale finds that these two "riddle" canons correspond to Quintilian's division of the argumentio into two sections: the probatio and the refutatio. Her structural analysis probes the extent to which the second canon, representing the refutatio, answers the "accusations" (probatio) of the first of the canon pair: "Since accusation is simpler," Quintilian notes, the first canon is but half the length of the second and has but

half the voices (four in the second). Because "defence needs a thousand
deviations and arts," in Quintilian's words, the second canon is the
longest one in the Musical Offering (excluding the Fuga Canonica) and
also the only one in four parts. Thus, it possesses the greatest variety
of simultaneous rhythms and melodies. The imitation by contrary motion
in the "accusation" canon may be intended to represent the adversary
relationship of the two sections of the rhetorical argumentio. Thus,
Quintilian says, "Our opponent is usually attacked by nearly the same
means, but inverted."(33)

Kirkendale's approach effectively reclaims one reading of Bach's
score. However, it may be claimed that in this score, Bach used several
deep, interconnecting associations whose intellectual content is difficult to recover. Sometimes the musico-intellectual commentary can be
reformulated with regard to Bach's intellectual milieu.   Read as a
Baroque document, the Musical Offering presents a musical iconography in
which the entire sequence of its thirteen sections, as well as smaller
musical entities such as phrase and polyphonic form, convey ideas. Indeed, Bach has superimposed multiple structures on his Musical Offering,
not an unusual practice in Baroque and Rococo art. Moreover, the various
structures of the work (the autobiographical and oratorical structures
among them), form a harmonious and interactive system of ideas. One need
not select a master or preeminent structure. Indeed, one cannot do so
because the manuscripts offer no conclusive evidence for the sequence and
there is disagreement over the sequence of some sections within the
Musical Offering.

For instance, whereas David and others arrange the ten canons into
two sets of five, neither Wolff nor Kirkendale accepts David's disposition.   Nonetheless, intellectual considerations can equally justify
David's centric organization of the sonata flanked by two sets of five
canons.   In addition to the arguments provided in David's work, other
considerations justify his arrangement.(34)

Of centralized symmetrical patterns, Alastair Fowler notes, "In the
baroque style, such ideas might be applied politically, as in the cult of
the Roi soleil."(35) As Baroque poetry, so Baroque music displays grand
centric orderings. Fowler provides several reasons for such design. He
notes, "The spatial tendency of Renaissance thought facilitated direct
control of formal organization by ideas; and conventions of centralized
symmetry naturally carried over from political protocol [e.g., triumphs
and pageants] into poetry, as they did into architecture."(36) Moreover,
the number five is the sovereign number, according to some traditions,
(37) and centric design around the number five, displays and echoes its
royal symbolism: the sonata, two ricercari, and two canon groups; the
two sets of five canons each; and the sonata's internal structure as
studied by David.(38)   Here we also find the Renaissance concept of the
parts echoing the whole design. Fowler cited Vitruvius's discussion of
architectural symmetry, with "the correspondence of each detail to the
form of the design as a whole."(39) Thus, monarchical symbolism is one
referent of the Musical Offering's structure.

Still, although Wolff has also cited royal symmetry as one reason
for centering the [sonata] in the Musical Offering's sequence of parts,
Kirkendale has argued that "axial symmetry must give way to considerations not only of rhetoric, but also of correct protocol. The royal ensemble sonata assumes the place of honor as a grand finale."(40) More
to her point, Kirkendale places the sonata last because, in her view, it
imitates the peroratio of Quintilian's oration.

The Musical Offering is an important document in the history of
ideas. Although instrumental works can be important as intellectual documents, this importance usually remains unnoticed because of the difficulty of extrapolating verbal or intellectual sense from sound. In Bach's
case, here and elsewhere among his works, the relationship between music,

words, and mathematics helps in the task. The seventeenth century had been a period of mathematical revolution. It was Johannes Kepler's mathematics and Galileo Galilei's astronomical model that helped to demonstrate the possibility of an infinite universe. In addition, Gottfried Leibniz's calculus gave mathematical form to the acceleration concept in Kepler's astronomical model. On the conservative side (never unimportant for a consideration of Bach's summative achievement), the symbolism and quantification charts of astrology were still very much in use. It was a great age for mathematics, and advances in that field continued throughout Bach's lifetime. One may ask whether Bach's allusion to the intellectual revolution of his time was ever more apparent than in the mathematical symbolism of the Musical Offering. As has been argued above, its structure representin an analogy for Bach's composition of the piece. In addition, the structure of the Musical Offering offers an analogy to his era's prevailing cosmological model. Hence we find the presence of the mathematics of infinity in the canon per tonos. It is fascinating to find, among Bach's works, such concern with a form for infinity, as though suggesting that new scientific concepts only seem to challenge God's circular plan. In the Musical Offering, the symmetrical and the asymmetrical coexist. Bach's musical message is one of spiritual cohesion and, in this respect, it resembles Galileo's attempts to retain the circular orbits of the planets, or Kepler's efforts to retain the earth's central position within the universe. Form itself always means something.

Manfred Bukofzer recognized this referential and "allegorical" tendency, referring to Baroque music as "subordinated to words and serving only as musical means to a dramatic end that transcended music."(41) More recently, Eric Chafe studied Bach's canons as Symbola. He wrote, "Allegorical art thus has an eschatological character according to which a more complete, fulfilled version of the work lies beyond what can be realized immediately in sound according to the written notes."(42)

As with Baroque music, so it was with Baroque literature of the seventeenth century. In Milton's Paradise Lost, for instance, we find the new Copernican astronomical model alongside the older, Ptolemaic representation. Milton uses either model to suit his purposes. In Paradise Lost, we also find the figure of Satan ranging through an enlarged space, treated on a larger scale than in any previous Western epic. Milton's treatment of space is, in respect to scale, like that of the Baroque painter Peter Paul Rubens, whose swirling movements extend the reader's eye throughout the dynamized painting, and whose jutting human limbs extend out from the canvas, and into the viewer's space. As the formal limits of Rubens's canvas dissolve, the observers are themselves pulled into his paintings. Thus, in assessing the Musical Offering manuscript, the decoding mind moves into the forms of Bach's music and thereby plays an active role in puzzling out the structure and its parts. To rephrase this idea, one might say that the listener's role includes active participation within the compositional space or the musical notation itself. In Baroque art and literature, space had indeed become infinite. In the Musical Offering, infinity received its formal treatment within the forms and implications of the music.

Paul Murray Kendall, in The Art of Biography, defines biography as "the simulation, in words, of a man's life, from all that is known about that man." He continues, "The shape of biography is partly created by the inner tensions peculiar to the practice."(43)   My contention has been that, in the Musical Offering, we have a simulation of several tensions, or oppositions, in Bach's life and art, handled both playfully and seriously. It may be that music's inherent plasticity is better suited to capture the feeling of such oppositions than is the verbal medium of autobiography. In the Musical Offering, we hear music whose form suggests specific life struggles, a tracing of Bach's life as subject of king and Church.   Such signatures are not unusual in music, but the polish by which Bach turned autobiography into music is unusual and, in its way, touching.

NOTES

1. Hans T. David and Arthur Mendel, eds., The Bach Reader (New York: W. W. Norton and Co., 1945), pp. 4-6.

2. Johann Nicolaus Forkel, On Johann Sebastian Bach's Life, Genius, and Works. Tr. disputed. In The Bach Reader, pp. 305-6.

3. David and Mendel, Bach Reader, pp. 6-7.

4. Douglas Hofstadter, Gödel Escher, Bach: An Eternal Golden Braid (New York: Random House, 1980), p. 1.

5. Ibid., p. 7.

6. Ibid.

7. Ibid.

8. Christoph Wolff, "New Research on Bach's Musical Offering," The Musical Quarterly 57 (1971): 391-95.

9. Hofstadter, Gödel, Escher, Bach, pp. 8-9.

10. Bach's use of the concept of infinity, a key motif in Hofstadter's Gödel, Escher, Bach, is studied later in my essay. J. J. Walther has written a Canone infinito gradato a 4 voci, sopra A solis ortus cardine. This canon appears in an autograph book containing a Bach Infinite Canon in Four Parts (see David and Mendel, Bach Reader, pp. 64-65).

11. Wolff, pp. 401-3.

12. Diagram developed from Hans Theodore David, Musical Offering: History, Interpretation, and Analysis (New York: Dover, 1972), p. 35. As is evident in my elaboration of the diagram, David argues that each of the two groups of canons mirrors the larger structure of the Musical Offering (pp. 35-37). However, the manuscripts do not present the canons in David's sequence; furthermore, some critics dispute David's solution to the problem of the work's unity.

13. Similar interrelationships appear among the two sets of canons (see David, Musical Offering, pp. 35-37).

14. David, Musical Offering, p. 110.

15. Wolff, "New Research," p. 400.

16. David, Musical Offering, p. 122.

17. This is only the beginning of the complicated symmetrical orderings very fully examined by David (Musical Offering, pp. 115-34).

18. Ibid., pp. 151-52.

19. Ibid., p. 23.

20. Philip Spitta, Johann Sebastian Bach, Tr. Clara Bell and J. A. Fuller-Maitland, Vol. 2 (London: Novello and Co. 1884-1885), p. 293.

21. Wolff, "New Research," p. 397ff.

22. Ibid., p. 407.

23. Ibid.

24. Ibid., p. 408.

25. Ibid.

26. Ursula Kirkendale notes that there have appeared about two dozen published arrangements of the components. She presents a comprehensive review of research on the manuscripts and the arrangements of the work's sections; see Ursula Kirkendale, "The Source for Bach's Musical Offering: The Institutio Oratoria of Quintilian," Journal of the American Musicological Society 33 (1980): 88-96.

27. Ibid.

28. Ibid., p. 131. Marcus Fabius Quintilianus died somewhat before the first century A.D. His Institutio Oratoria is available in Latin with a facing English translation in the Loeb Classical Library, tr. H.E. Butler, 4 vols. (Cambridge: Harvard UP, 1921 and subsequent reprints). Kirkendale used the London printing: William Heinemann, 1933-36.

29. Ibid., p. 132.

30. Kirkendale's quotation comes from Johann Scheibe, Critsicher Musikus (Leipzig, 1745), p. 997.

31. Quintilian, Institutio, V.xii.1), cited in Kirkendale, "Source," p. 119.

32. Christoph Wolff, Kritischer Bericht (Kassel, 1976), p. 106, cited in Kirkendale, "Source," p. 119.

33. Quintilian, Institutio, IV.i.14, V.xiii.1-2, cited in Kirkendale, "Source," pp. 119-20.

34. David, Musical Offering, pp. 34-43, 111-34.

35. Alastair Fowler, Triumphal Forms: Structural Patterns in Elizabethan Poetry (Cambridge: Cambridge University Press, 1970), p. 119.

36. Ibid., p. 62.

37. Ibid., pp. 25-26.

38. David, Musical Offering, pp. 6-8.

39. Vitruvius De archit., I.ii.4., cited in Fowler, Triumphal Forms, p. 99.

40. Kirkendale, "Source," p. 121.

41. Manfred Bukofzer, "Allegory in Baroque Music," Journal of the Warburg and Courtauld Institutes 3 (1939-1940): 8.

42. Eric Chafe, "Allegorical Music: The Symbolism of Tonal Language in the Bach Canons," Journal of Musicology 3 (1984): 342.

43. Paul Murray Kendall, The Art of Biography (New York: W. W. Norton, 1965), p. 15.

8

Bach and Edwards on the Religious Affections

Richard A. Spurgeon Hall

And David and all the house of Israel played before the
Lord on all manner of instruments made of fir wood, even   on harps,
and on psalteries, and on timbrels, and on cornets, and on cymbals.
(2 Sam. 6:5)

Linking Johann Sebastian Bach, the Lutheran cantor, with Jonathan Edwards, the Reformed divine, might be greeted with some surprise given
Calvinism's anathema of concerted church music.   After all, did not
Calvin ban the performance of polyphonic and instrumental music during
divine service?   Did not Puritans banish all but the chanting of metrical
psalms from English churches during the Commonwealth, thereby bringing
about the demise of the indigenous and venerable institution of sacred
music in England?   Indeed, is not the Puritan's niggardly attitude toward
liturgical music epitomized in an eighteenth century Dissenting minister's remark that "instrumental music is not fit and proper for the public worship of God," with the justification that "the Christian religion
shines brightest in its own dress; and to paint it is to deform it"? (1)
Happily, Edwards is a conspicuous exception to this Puritanic rule of
music phobia. On the contrary, he had a relish for music. (2) There is
even evidence in his thought of a nascent aesthetics of music in which
that art is accorded not only a devotional use and a moral purpose, but a
metaphysical significance as well. (3)
     Edwards can be compared with Bach, though, through more than a
shared musical aesthetic. Apart from the obvious, their contemporaneity
and comparable preeminence in the service of their common faith--the one
the greatest theologian and the other the greatest church musician of his
age, both were associated with conservative Protestant movements of spiritual renewal that stressed the centrality of personal experience and
feeling in religion: Edwards with Evangelicalism and Bach (albeit ambiv-
alently) with Pietism. Each approached the mystical in the intensity of
his devoutness, and both undertook to spread the gospel in ways suitable
to their vocations: Bach as a composer and performer, and Edwards as a
theologian and preacher. Each, in his espousal of a palpable orthodoxy,
went against the currents of rationalism, skepticism, and infidelity ram-
pant in the eighteenth century. Nonetheless, both appealed to reason,
seeking a fusion of thought and emotion that went beyond the narrower
rationalism of a Christian Wolff or Gottfried Leibniz.   Edwards, who
early on had eagerly assimilated Isaac Newton and John Locke, and was no
less enlightened than Denis Diderot,(4) demonstrated that the understanding is as crucial to true religion as the emotions, that even the mysteries of the Christian faith are in principle explicable, and that God is
knowable through a kind of affective cognition, whereas Bach, even in his
simplest pedagogical pieces, united head and heart in music that, in its
peerless logic, fully exemplifies Boethius's conception of music as aural
mathematics while still managing to be poignantly affective.   Though
never lacking some contemporary admirers, neither man was fully understood and appreciated in his own time, each having to await a posthumous

acclaim--Bach until the nineteenth century, and Edwards until the twentieth.   Finally, both in a way were tragic figures, religious visionaries
of sorts whose schemes were thwarted.   Edwards's attempt to transform his
congregation into a community of saints actually practicing the faith
they professed was foiled by his dismissal at their hands.   Bach's en-
deavor to institute at St. Thomas's Church   "a well-regulated church
music, to the glory of God" was rebuffed by his indifferent superiors.
    Associating Bach and Edwards is worthwhile for three reasons.   One
is that it allows us to see their reinforcement of one another.   Indivi-
dually, each appears to have been a somewhat solitary and reactionary
figure at odds with the severely rationalistic and heterodox spirit of
the age.   Edwards vigilantly warned against and strenuously opposed the
encroaching Deism, Arminianism, and other threats to Orthodoxy in the New
England churches, whereas Bach chafed under the regimen of the rational-
ist Johann August Ernesti, the rector of St. Thomas School where Bach was
employed, who sought to reform the curriculum by demoting music on the
grounds that it was anti-intellectual.(5)   Moreover, he ran afoul of the
rationalistic aesthetics of Johann Adolph Scheibe, who censured him for
writing overly complex music.(6)   Jointly, however, Bach and Edwards can
be seen to have formed an imposing counterpoint to some dominant themes
of the Enlightenment.   Second reason is that associating Bach and Edwards
allows each to enhance our understanding and appreciation of the other.
Thus, Edwards, through his theological aesthetic, can clarify for us
Bach's conception of music, even suggesting how we should listen to it;
while Bach, through his compositions, shows us that Edwards's aesthetic
has not only theoretical interest but also a practical application in the
arts.   A third reason is that Edwards may provide a clue to the resolution of a contentious issue in Bach scholarship by enabling us to understand how Bach, far from losing his faith, may have rethought it (as did
Edwards); and to see that the more conservative style of some of Bach's
late sacred works may be the fruit of a profounder and more sophisticated
spirituality.
    The focus of this chapter is, specifically, Bach and Edwards's com-
mon conception of the emotions--or "affections" in eighteenth century
parlance--as an essential element in both music and religion, and as the
link between them.   Edwards considered the emotions essential to genuine
religion, and both he and Bach shared the contemporary opinion that a
function of music is to elicit human emotion.   They thought, therefore,
that music, by eliciting the specifically "religious" emotions in the
listener, would help make him or her more pious.   We shall show that Bach
and Edwards complement one another inasmuch as the latter's theory of the
religious affections provides a theological rationale for Bach's poignantly affecting religious music, whereas Bach's music seems to presup-
pose, and certainly is compatible with, something like Edwards's concept
of religion, and fully conforms to his theological precepts for music.

I

    Doubts about Bach's devoutness and about the veracity of the
admittedly romanticized portraits of him as the fifth evangelist or the
spiritual grandson of Martin Luther have recently been raised by the
disclosure that in later life he virtually gave up composing music for
the church.   This was made through Alfred Dürr's and Georg von Dadelsen's
new chronologies of Bach's works showing that the Leipzig cantatas came
largely from the early years of Bach's cantorate there.   Spurred on by
these findings, Friedrich Blume sought to discredit Bach's presumed
religiosity.   He argued that Bach was not a cantor from religious con-
viction, and that his church compositions were "half-willing, half-
unwilling contributions."(7)   However, Dürr himself replied, "Bach was a
pious but not fanatical Lutheran who considered the performance of every

duty to be in the service of God, whether it was that of organist, court musician or Cantor."(8)   Support for Dürr has come of late from the discovery in 1969 of Bach's own copy of Johann Abraham Calov's edition of Luther's Bible with its extensive marginalia and underlinings (authenticated as Bach's) attesting to his serious study of Scripture. Particularly noteworthy are the interpolated passages in First Book of Chronicles (Chapters 26 and 29) concerned with music in the temple.(9) These suggest that Bach took church music and the office of cantor seriously enough to seek for them a divine sanction. "Above all," writes Gerhard Herz, "the Calov Bible proves what has always been assumed on the basis of Bach's church music, namely, that Bach was a profoundly devout person who not only knew and read his Bible but related his professional life, work and position to it."(10)

Why, then, did Bach virtually abandon the composition of sacred cantatas a scant four years after his appointment in Leipzig? Herz's plausible explanation is that Bach had become discouraged by disputes over salary and prerogative with his unappreciative employers, and so, typically, composed less for them. "When he had to fight for certain rights and privileges, the flood of his weekly cantata output dried up." The evidence suggests, then, that in mid-life Bach virtually abandoned the composition of sacred cantatas not from a crisis in or lack of faith, but, on the contrary, from a faith intense enough to seek vocational expression and to thereby incur that antagonism between him and the authorities that led to his disillusionment. "Bach's recurrent and keen disappointment was not in his faith but in its earthly representatives. With them he fought endless battles; at them he was, as we now can say, angry in nomine Domini."(11)   Furthermore, though Bach slackened his production of music for the Lutheran service, he by no means quit composing religious music. In his last years he revised his Passions, completed and integrated the Mass in B Minor, and composed the short masses, the Schübler Chorales, the Eighteen Chorales, and the Canonic Variations on the Christmas Song, "Vom Himmel hoch da komm ich her."

There can be no doubt, however, about Bach's avowed intention in composing. Bach regarded musical composition as an act of devotion, and sought to glorify God in even the technical details of the art. In a paraphrase for his students of F. E. Niedt's book on thoroughbass, Bach stated unequivocally--echoing Luther--that "the aim and final reason, as of all music, so of the thoroughbass should be none else but the Glory of God and the recreation of the mind. Where this is not observed, there will be no real music but only a devilish hubbub."(12)

Consistent with that aim, Bach routinely initialed the first and last pages of the scores of his church music with J.J. (Jesu, Juva: Jesus help) and S. D. G. (Soli Deo Gloria: To God alone the glory) respectively. He similarly inscribed the scores of his secular, even pedagogical, compositions. Thus, the Clavier-Büchlein, written for the instruction of his son Wilhelm Friedemann, carries the inscription I. N. J. (In Nomine Jesu: In the name of Jesus).(13) Bach made no real distinction, then, between sacred and profane music; for him, all music, whatever its immediate function, should ultimately serve a devotional end, an aesthetic creed that Albert Schweitzer summarized as follows: "Music is an act of worship with Bach. All great art, even secular, is in itself religious in his eyes; for him the tones do not perish, but ascend to God like praise too deep for utterance." (14)

With Bach, music is also a vehicle for evangelism, something Luther recognized in saying, "St. Paul encouraged the use of music in order that through it the word of God and Christian doctrine might be preached, taught, and put into practice."(15) Through music the Word can be proclaimed graphically and affectingly. Thus, to this end, Bach devised a highly articulate and complex tonal language for symbolizing Christian doctrines and depicting biblical episodes.

In Bach's musical exegesis of Scripture, the meaning of the texts becomes something to be not merely understood but experienced by the listeners; something that grasps and moves them, inviting their emotional response. Jan Chiapusso describes this process as follows: "Bach's musical Bibelauslegung, or pictorial explanation of the Bible, combines the creation of a visual image in the mind's eye with the emotional essence of its idea."(16) Examples of such affective aural picturing abound in Bach's church cantatas. One striking example is the soprano aria of Cantata 11, "Lobet Gott in seinen Reichem" ("Praise God in His Kingdom"). This piece vividly conveys the idea of the Ascension by conjuring up for the mind's eye a suitable visual image. High-pitched instruments, two flutes and an oboe whose melodies are unsupported by an earth-bound thoroughbass, create the illusion of height; while sequences of undulating sixteenth notes suggest the billowing clouds behind which Christ eventually disappears. Throughout, the music itself expresses rapture, conveying the emotional essence of the theological idea.

What interests us here is the expression of emotion in Bach's tonal picturing of a religious idea. His music perfectly illustrates the eighteenth century Affektenlehre, or "doctrine of the affections," according to which the function of music is to express the affections (emotions, feelings, moods, etc.) or to "paint the passions." J. G. Ziegler, a student of Bach attests to his teacher's scrupulousness in the precise musical rendering of the affective purport of language: "As concerns the playing of chorales, I was instructed by my teacher, Capellmeister Bach, who is still living, not to play the songs merely offhand but according to the sense [affect] of the words."(17) More recently, Jan Chiapusso has commented in a similar vein on Bach's faithfulness to the meaning of the hymn text in the composition of chorale preludes: "Bach considered the content of the words of each hymn of foremost importance and he used a great variety of musical motives, rhythmical and ornamental figures, and descriptive intervals to illustrate the text."(18) The chorale prelude, "In dir Ist Freude" ("In Thee Is Joy") from his Orgelbüchlein is a case in point. Here Bach vigorously expresses jubilation through an insistent and recurrent dance-like motif in the bass, with garlands of eighth notes in the two upper voices. Especially significant is the fact that Bach was concerned with expressing intense emotion, thereby making his music maximally expressive, this is something on which Schweitzer remarked: "Bach is thus bent in making music characteristically expressive at any cost. Before he decides simply to write beautiful music to a text, he searches the words through and through to find an emotion which, after it has been intensified, is suitable for musical representation."(19)

As an example of the fervency of Bach's vocal music, consider the rhapsodic violin obbligato accompanying the "Laudamus Te" of his Mass in B Minor. It is noteworthy, however, that those of Bach's late religious compositions reverting to the Palestrina style of the sixteenth century are less fervent and more impersonal and detached, expressing as they do "the severe and rather abstract affect of majestas or gravitas--the one furthest removed from the passionate affects that had become the sine qua non in the Baroque household of emotions."(20)

What theological rationale, though, can be given for Bach's intentness on and care in expressing fervid emotions musically? May the subdued affective character of some of his late sacred music be theologically significant? Might this reflect Bach's spiritual maturation? Answers can be found, I think, in Jonathan Edwards, and coming as they do from surely the greatest theologian in the English-speaking world, to be brought to bear on the work of perhaps the greatest composer, they have a special significance. The theological rationale is implicit in Edwards's theory of religion, to the consideration of which I shall now turn.

II

Throughout his life, Edwards was exercised by the perennial question as to the nature of true religion, or the essence of Christianity. He admitted that this was "a subject on which my mind has been peculiarly intent, ever since I first entered on the study of divinity," and that there was "no question whatsoever, that is of greater importance to mankind."(21) This was corroborated by Samuel Hopkins, Edwards's disciple and first biographer, who wrote that "Perhaps none has taken more pains, or labored more successfully"(22) over the question of true religion than Jonathan Edwards. A later commentator, John E. Smith, even suggested that the whole of Edwards's thought might be construed as "one magnificent answer"(23) to this question.

If Smith is right, then the first sustained and most systematic stage of Edwards's answer is in his A Treatise Concerning Religious Affections (1746). One of his aims in this treatise was to defend the crucial role of the emotions in religion against those like Charles Chauncy, a fellow Congregationalist minister, who, alarmed by the unbridled emotionalism and fanaticism of the "Great Awakening," would banish them entirely, thereby reducing religion to a matter wholly of reason and--ultimately--inactivity.(24) For Edwards, however, not any kind of emotion is authentically religious. Another of his aims, then, was to furnish a set of criteria--what he called "signs"--whereby genuinely "holy affections" might be distinguished from those that were spuriously so, lest religion be reduced to the hysteria and undisciplined "enthusiasm" of a James Davenport, a contemporary evangelist.(25)

Edwards's motto for the treatise is a quotation from a letter of the Apostle Peter to his persecuted brethren, whom he addresses as follows: "Whom having not seen, ye love: in whom, though now ye see him not, yet believing, ye rejoice with joy unspeakable, and full of glory" (1 Peter 1:8).(26) Thus described is religion under trial. This Edwards considered exemplary because, as he observed, religion is at its very best under such circumstances. Tribulation purifies religion and proves unmistakably its truth and merit, just as fire refines gold and assays its genuineness and worth. Such is the case with the faith described by Peter. It has been vindicated inasmuch as those who were animated by it remain loyal to Christ throughout their afflictions, not only steadfastly, but joyfully so.

Edwards notes as significant that the Apostle characterizes the religion of the Christians he addresses as operating in the form of emotional states--conspicuously, love and joy:

> We see that the Apostle, in observing and remarking the
> operations and exercises of religion, in the Christians he
> wrote to, singles out the religious affections of love and
> joy, wherein their religion did thus appear true and pure,
> and in its proper glory.

And the joy is described as "unspeakable," no less, both in kind--being "very different from worldly joys, and carnal delights; of a vastly more pure, sublime and heavenly nature"--and in degree--"it pleasing God to give 'em this holy joy, with a liberal hand, and in large measure, in their state of persecution." It is further described as a joy "full of glory" which Edwards interprets as "a most worthy, noble rejoicing, that did not corrupt and debase the mind, as many carnal joys do; but did greatly beautify and dignify it." From this, Edwards infers that "true religion, in great part, consists in holy affections."(27)

Before establishing this claim, Edwards explains what he means by "affections." What he refers to as "affections" we refer to, less precisely, as emotions or feelings. He conceives affections as "the more

vigorous and sensible exercises" of the will. The will is that faculty
by which the mind, in his words, "is some way inclined with respect to
the things it views or considers; either is inclined to ´em, or is disin-
clined, and averse from ´em." In this capacity, the mind "does not behold things, as an indifferent unaffected spectator, but either as liking
or disliking, please or displeased, approving or rejecting." In some
cases, the mind "is carried but a little beyond a state of perfect in-
difference" with respect to what it views; but in others, it "comes to
act vigorously and sensibly." These latter actions or exercises of the
will are what Edwards calls "affections." For Edwards, then, "the
affections are not essentially distinct from the will," and differ from
volitions "only in the liveliness and sensibleness of exercise":

> In every act of the will whatsoever, the soul either likes or
> dislikes, is either inclined or disinclined to what is in
> view: these are not essentially different from those affec-
> tions of love and hatred: that liking or inclination of the
> soul to a thing, if it be in a high degree, and be vigorous
> and lively, is the very same thing with the affection of
> love: and that disliking and disinclining, if in a great
> degree, is the very same with hatred.(28)

Affections and volitions occupy the same continuum of inclination. The
only difference between them is that volition is "inclination expressed
in action" whereas affection is "inclination expressed in the mind." (29)
     That genuine religion is largely affectional, Edwards thinks, is
sufficiently established from his conception of the affections. The genuinely religious mind is anything but indifferent or unaffected; indeed,
it is characteristically devoted and zealous--or, in Edwards´s analysis,
strongly inclined or attracted to its objects. "In nothing, is vigor in
the actings of our inclinations so requisite, as in religion," affirmed
Edwards, "and in nothing is lukewarmness so odious."   Since for Edwards,
such vigorous exercises of inclination are in fact affections, then religion is chiefly characterized by them: "Wherever true religion is,
there are vigorous exercises of the inclination and will towards divine
objects: but by what was said before, the vigorous, lively and sensible
exercises of the will, are no other than the affections of the soul."(30)
     Edwards, however, did adduce further reasons to support his claim
that emotions are essential to genuine religion. One is that religious
affections are a necessary condition for the existence of religious behavior, without which religion is merely a matter of ineffectual belief
and idle reflection; classically stated, such affections are necessary
for works, without which faith is dead. Edwards´s explanation was that,
since affections give impetus to human behavior--"such is man´s nature,
that he is very inactive, any otherwise than he is influenced by some
affection" so the specifically religious affections give impetus to religious behavior, the hallmark of genuine religion: "And as in worldy
things, worldly affections are very much the spring of men´s motion and
action; so in religious matters, the spring of their actions are very
much religious affections: he that has doctrinal knowledge and specula-
tion only, without affection, never is engaged in the business of
religion."(31)
     A second reason is that the experience of a religious conversion
(the sine qua non of true piety), or becoming religious, is at all possible only by our being "affected" or moved by the things of religion:
"the things of religion take hold of men´s souls, no further than they
affect them."(32)
     A third reason is that, according to Scripture, sin consists largely
of hardness of heart, or emotional unresponsiveness to the things of religion, which means the lack of religious affections. By contrast, then,

argued Edwards, piety must consist largely in tenderness of heart, or susceptibility to spiritual things, which is the tendency to having such affections:

> Now therefore since it is so plain, that by a hard heart, in Scripture, is meant a heart destitute of pious affections, and since also the Scriptures do so frequently place the sin and corruption of the heart in hardness of heart; it is evident, that the grace and holiness of the heart, on the contrary, must, in great measure, consist in its having pious affections, and being easily susceptive of such affection.(33)

Finally, a fourth reason, and one of particular interest to us, is "the nature and design of the ordinances and duties" God has chosen "as means and expressions of true religion." One such duty cited by Edwards is, notably, the glorification of God through music. The purpose of glorifying God musically, according to Edwards, is to both express and evoke religious emotions, functions that music performs so effectively:

> And the duty of singing praises to God, seems to be appointed wholly to excite and express religious affections. No other reason can be assigned, why we should express ourselves to God in verse, rather than in prose, and do it with music, but only, that such is our nature and frame, that these things have a tendency to move our affections.(34)

As we have indicated, Edwards furnished criteria, or "signs," whereby truly spiritual emotions or affections might be distinguished from the speciously so and, since the former are essential to authentic faith, whereby true religion might be distinguished from false. We shall now look at the ninth, tenth, and twelfth of Edwards's twelve signs of holiness in affections (and, thus, signs of the genuineness of faith), which are the ones relevant to our purpose.

Edwards listed as the ninth sign, whereby the genuineness of religious affections might be known, one of the affections' effects; namely, their making for tenderness of heart, a hallmark of genuine Christianity: "Gracious affections soften the heart, and are attended and followed with a Christian tenderness of spirit."(35) He variously described this tenderness as susceptibility to the influence of spiritual things; sympathy; a propensity for being moved by acts of kindness, and for grief and alarm over moral evil; a lack of self-confidence during spiritual danger, depending instead on Christ; acute awareness of and vigilance against moral temptations; a dread of divine wrath; and an awe and reverence in approaching God.

Edwards's tenth sign is the relationship among holy affections, which is harmony: "Another thing wherein those affections that are truly gracious and holy, differ from those that are false, is beautiful symmetry and proportion." They are harmonious, for Edwards, when none is neglected or exercised at the expense of another, with each being given its due exercise, and complementing the others. Such is the case with the real Christian, or the saint, but not the hypocrite: "There is in many of them [hypocrites] a great partiality, with regard to the several kinds of religious affections: great affections in some things, and no manner of proportion in others. In the saints, joy and holy fear go together. But many of these [hypocrites] rejoice without trembling.(36)

His last sign of genuinely religious affections is another of their effects; namely, their issuing in good works: "Holy affections have their exercise and fruit in Christian practice." Edwards considered this the most compelling sign or evidence of holiness, the confirmation and consummation of the rest: "Christian practice is the most proper evidence

evidence of the gracious sincerity of professors, to themselves and others; and the chief of all the marks of grace, the sign of signs, and evidence of evidences, that which seals and crowns all other signs."(37) Indeed, he devoted far more space to this discussion than to that of any of the other signs, testimony to the supreme importance he attaches to it.

I am prepared now to derive a theological rationale for the passion- ateness of Bach's sacred music from Edwards's conception of true religion as being affectional in nature; particularly, from some of his reasons for attributing true religion to the affections, and from some of his criteria for determining their holiness.

Now if affections of a certain kind are constitutive of true piety, and music, does, in Edwards's words, "have a tendency to move our affect- ions," then it must have a tendency to affect us spiritually as well. Specifically, said Edwards, "Music, especially sacred music, has a power- ful efficacy to soften the heart into tenderness, to harmonize the affections, and to give the mind a relish for objects of a superior character."(38)   Inasmuch as music produces these effects in us, it directly fosters the very qualities of true religion that Edwards pain- stakingly describes in his treatise. Thus, by softening our hearts, music makes us less prone to sin through hardness of heart, making in- stead for that "Christian tenderness of spirit" that is Edwards's ninth sign of authentic faith. By harmonizing our affections, music makes for that "beautiful symmetry and proportion" among them which is the tenth sign.   By enabling the mind to relish more elevated objects, such as those of the spirit, music increases our susceptibility to them and thereby our tendency toward religion. As Edwards said: "The things of religion take hold of men's souls, no further than they affect them." Ultimately and most important, by stirring our religious affections, music sets in motion the spring of religious actions, thereby, perhaps, leading to good works, the twelfth sign.

Edwards's theological rationale for sacred music, then, is that it makes for true religion by influencing the emotions in the ways described above: "The duty of singing praises to God, seems to be appointed wholly to excite and express religious affections."   And it serves especially well as a rationale for the sacred music of Bach, in particular, for the following reasons: For one thing, Bach fulfills what Edwards understands to be the sole purpose of sacred music, which is "to excite and express religious affections."   Indeed, his church music excites and expresses, to an extraordinary degree of intensity and subtlety, the gamut of re- ligious affections, thereby producing, presumably, the emotional and spiritual effects described by Edwards. For another, Bach would undoubt- edly have sympathized with the kind of piety Edwards prescribed in his treatise on religious affections--if he did not in fact exemplify it himself.   Edwards's conception of affectional piety is akin to that espoused by Pietism,(39) the movement of spiritual renewal within the Lutheran Church inaugurated by Philipp J. Spener in the late seventeenth century and which continued to exert its influence down to Bach's own day, which too "made claims for the affective and sometimes also the conative aspects of religion, in devotion and in practical service."(40) Bach was sympathetic to the spirit, if not the letter, of Pietism.(41) He routinely set cantata texts by Salomon Franck and Erdmann Neumeister which are full of Pietistic sentiments. Moreover, his precise and palpable expression in music of the spiritual core of these texts is something fully in accord with Pietism:

It is Pietism that inspires Bach's attitude toward the re- ligious text that is to be transformed into music. It is Pietism that accounts for his unswerving resolve to approach the concealed meaning of the word, for his devout contempla-

tion of the religious value inherent in the word, and for his
anxiety to do full justice to the word whose religious con-
notations the artistic form must not injure.(42)

However, what of the theological significance of the more austere
and abstract emotional character of those of Bach's late religious works,
which are cast in the antique style? This may be suggested by Edwards's
later conception of the religious affections, which seems reminiscent of
Herz's characterization of the affections expressed in these works.
According to his Religious Affections, the primary motive of a truly
religious love is the moral virtue of the beloved: "[Holy persons] love
God, in the first place, for the beauty of his holiness or moral perfection."(43) Love so motivated Edwards would later call "love of complacence," which is "delight...in the person or being beloved for his [moral]
beauty." However, according to his later The Nature of True Virtue, the
primary motive of a truly virtuous love is existence as such: "The first
object of a virtuous benevolence is being, simply considered." This means
that God is to be loved principally not for his holiness, but for himself
alone. Love so motivated Edwards calls "love of benevolence," which is
that "propensity of the heart to any being, which...disposes it to desire
and take pleasure in its happiness."(44)
Benevolence, since it involves one's being happy in another's happiness, might be described as a second-order emotion, one that is disinter-
ested, impersonal, reflective--in a word, abstract--and (presumably) less
fervid than complacence. Also less fervid are the emotions flowing from
benevolence in contrast to those flowing from complacence, for in
Edwards's psychology, love is "the chief of the affections, and fountain
of all other affections."(45) Consequently, the affection of benevolence
imparts to the religious life an emotional tone more subdued than the
affection of complacence.
Edwards's reconception of religious affections marks a shift from a
basically subjectivist ethic, whose ultimate norm is our humanity's own
happiness, to an objectivist ethic, whose ultimate norm is God's happiness; and a shift from a basically anthropocentric ethic, where God is
loved primarily for the pleasure--however spiritual--he gives us, to a
radically theocentric ethic, where God is loved primarily for his own
sake.
Now benevolence, along with the religious affections it engenders,
seems somewhat analogous in character to "the severe and rather abstract
affect of majestas or gravitas" expressed by Bach's later music in the
old style. Might the emotional austerity and abstruseness of this music
be theologically significant insofar as they represent an objectivism and
theocentrism on Bach's part as well? These qualities are certainly
evident in the sacred works of his last period. Thus, Bach's preference
late in life for setting the Latin Mass with its objective doctrines and
the traditional Lutheran hymn texts, rather than (as earlier) the
vernacular religious poetry (usually Pietist) with its subjective and
emotionally charged sentiments, suggests an objectivist frame of mind
envisioning an art universal in scope rather than narrowly sectarian.
Furthermore, Bach's preoccupation during his last years with producing
works not intended for performance suggests a theocentric concern with
glorifying God before edifying his fellow men and women. "His last organ
chorale, 'Vor deinen Thron tret ich hiemit' ('I Herewith Step Before Thy
Throne'), makes the musician or scholar who dares to follow him to such
heights almost mystically aware that here Bach is alone with his
God."(46)
Finally, might the emotional severity and abstractness of Bach's
late corpus reflect a maturation in his faith? It would not be far-
fetched to suppose that the older Bach sought to distance himself from
such extremes of Pietism as excessive emotionalism, subjectivism,

escapism, and anti-intellectualism (just as Edwards sought to distance himself from "enthusiasm"), and that his music reflects this impulse in its emotive character.   Indeed, one wonders whether Bach and Edwards underwent a similar kind of spiritual metamorphosis.(47)

Bach's music and Edward's theology, then, are complementary, thereby enriching and illuminating each other: The one, by eliciting in us the specifically religious emotions with their spiritual concomitants-- thereby engaging us in the things of religion--invites and enables us to participate vicariously in the Christian life, a life of enhanced feeling and enriched experience, which the other describes and prescribes. With their common conception of religion and art as fundamentally matters of feeling, Bach and Edwards made room for religion, and religious music, in an age that had grown impatient with both.

NOTES

1. A Tractate of Church Music: being an Extract from the Reverend and Learned Mr. Peirce's Vindication of the Dissenters (London: 1786), quoted in Annals of King's Chapel (King's Chapel, Boston), p. 210.

2. Edwards seems to have been innately musical, finding song a natural means of privately expressing his innermost thoughts, ecstacies, and devotions. He related in his memoirs that as a youth he was wont to spend hours outdoors communing with God through nature while singing out his musings:
"I often used to sit and view the moon for a long time; and in the day, spent much time in viewing the clouds and sky, to behold the sweet glory of God in these things: in the meantime singing forth, with a low voice, my contemplations of the Creator and Redeemer. . . It always seem- ed natural for me to sing or chant forth my meditations; or, to speak my thoughts in soliloquies with a singing voice (The Works of President Edwards), ed. E. Hickman, vol. 1 London; 1834, p. xiii.

3. For Edwards, the harmony in music is the very image, or type, of divine love that obtains paradigmatically among the persons of the God- head, between God and his creatures, and among sanctified human beings: "When one thing sweetly harmonizes with another, as the notes in music, the notes are so conformed and have such proportion one to another, that they seem to have respect one to another as if they loved one another." That love, moreover, is what constitutes spiritual being and, more in- directly, physical being;   The Works of Jonathan Edwards, ed. Wallace Earl Anderson, vol. 6 (New Haven; 1980), p. 380.

4. The question of Edwards's relationship to the Enlightenment is difficult and controversial. For a full discussion, see John Opie, Jr., ed. Jonathan Edwards and the Enlightenment (Lexington, Mass: 1969).

5. For the primary documents pertaining to the quarrels between Bach and Ernesti, consult Hans David and Arthur Mendel; eds. The Bach Reader, 1st rev. ed. W. W. Norton (New York; 1966), pp. 137-58.

6. Scheibe was an organist and music critic who had studied under Bach and Johann Christoph Gottsched, a disciple of Christian Wolff and an exponent of the Enlightenment who taught at the University of Leipzig. Scheibe wrote, "This great man ⌊Bach⌋would be the admiration of whole nations if he had more amenity, if he did not take away the natural element in his pieces by giving them a turgid and confused style, and if he did not darken their beauty by an excess of art." David and Mendel; The Bach Reader, p. 238.

7. Ibid., p. 423.

8. Ibid.

9. Bach's note on 1 Chron. 25, the chapter describing David's pro-
vision for temple music, translates, "This chapter is the true foundation
of all church music pleasing to God." The translation of his comment on
Chron. 28:21, a verse implicitly including the services of musicians in
worship, reads, "Magnificent proof that, besides other functions of the
divine service, music especially has also been ordered into existence by
God's spirit through David." Significantly, Bach underlined with red ink
parts of verses 12 and 13 of 2 Chron. 5 which tell of God's glory in the
form of a cloud filling the sanctuary during the singing of the great
hymn that ushered in the Ark of the Covenant. Bach's remark in the margin translates, "In devotional music, God with his grace is always present." This and further information about Bach's Calov Bible are cited in
Gerhard Herz, "Essays on J. S. Bach," Studies in Musicology, vol. 73
(Ann Arbor, 1985); 158-63.

10. Ibid., p. 163.

11. Ibid., pp. 164, 170.

12. David and Mendel; The Bach Reader, p. 33. It is worth noting
that Bach's statement concerning the end of music is virtually identical
with one of Luther's from his Tabletalk: "The whole purpose of harmony
is the glory of God; all other use is but the idle juggling of Satan"
Wilfrid Mellers, Bach and the Dance of God; (New York, 1981), pp. 81-82.

13. Ibid., p. 32

14. Albert Schweitzer, J.S. Bach, tr. Ernest Newman, vol. 1 (London;
1935), p. 167.

15. Mellers, Dance of God, pp. 81-2.

16. Jan Chiapusso, Bach's World (Bloomington, Ind.; 1968), p. 207.

17. David and Mendel, The Bach Reader, p. 237.

18. Chiapusso, Bach's World, p. 201.

19. Schweitzer, J. S. Bach, vol. 2, p. 36.

20. Herz, "Essays", p. 174.

21. Jonathan Edwards, A Treatise Concerning Religious Affections, in
The Works of Jonathan Edwards, ed. John E. Smith, vol. 2 (New Haven;
1959), p. 84.

22. Samuel Hopkins, The Life and Character of the Late Reverend Mr.
Jonathan Edwards (Boston; 1765), repr. in David Levin; ed. Jonathan
Edwards: A Profile, American Profiles (New York; 1969), p. 2.

23. John E. Smith, "Editor's Introduction," in Jonathan Edwards,
Religious Affections, in the Works, vol. 2 (New Haven; 1959), p. 2.

24. Charles Chauncy (1705-1787) co-pastor of Boston's First Church,
was the intellectual leader of the anti-revival forces in eighteenth century New England. He dismissed the religiosity resulting from the revi-

vals as "the effect of enthusiastic heat."   Seasonable Thoughts on the
State of Religion in New England, a Treatise in Five Parts (Boston; 1743)
is Chauncy's rejoinder to Edwards' Some Thoughts Concerning the Present
Revival of Religion in New England (Boston; 1742), whose position he mis-
took for enthusiasm.   See Goen's "Editor's Introduction," pp. 61-4, 80-3.

25. James Davenport (1716-1757) was an especially virulent enthusi-
ast.   He was a text-book example of the religious vices that Edwards and
Chauncy concurred in deploring.   Davenport was censorious.   In the summer
of 1741, he went about Connecticut summoning ministers to give an account
to him of their conversion experiences.   Those that refused, being the
majority, he denounced publicly as apostate.   Davenport was a Separatist.
He urged congregations to abandon or dismiss "unconverted" pastors.   He
was also a fanatic.   On March 6, 1743, he led his followers to the wharf
at New London and exhorted them to renounce their "idolatrous love of
worldly things."   As a result, they stripped themselves of their finery,
wigs, and jewels, and burned them.   Thereafter, Davenport was arraigned
and declared non compos mentis.   See Goen, "Editor's Introduction," pp.
51-2, 60-1.

26. Edwards, Religious Affections, p. 93.

27. Ibid., p. 95.

28. Ibid., pp. 96-7.

29. Smith, "Editor's Introduction," p. 14.

30. Edwards, Religious Affections, p. 100.

31. Ibid., p. 101.

32. Ibid.

33. Ibid., p. 118.

34. Ibid., pp. 114-15.

35. Ibid., p. 357.

36. Ibid., pp. 365-66.

37. Ibid., pp. 383, 443.

38. Jonathan Edwards, Memoirs, in Hickman, Works of President
Edwards, vol. 1, p. cxxxviii.

39. Edwards knew of and sympathized with German Pietism, recognizing
it as kindred to the evangelical Calvinism he espoused.   In Some Thoughts
Concerning the Present Revival of Religion in New England, he cited
approvingly the efforts of August Hermann Francke on behalf of religion--
Francke was an eminent Pietist who held an appointment at the newly
founded University of Halle, and established both an orphanage and an in-
novative system of education: "If God's people in this land were once
brought to abound in such deeds of love, . . . it would be a most blessed
omen.   . . . And so it was in the late remarkable revival or religion in
Saxony, which began by the labours of the famous professor Franck [sic],
and has now been carried on for above thirty years, and has spread its
happy influences into many parts of the world."   Hickman; Works of President Edwards, vol. 1, p. 429.

40. Paul Edwards, ed. The Encyclopedia of Philosophy, vol. 6 (New York; 1967), p. 168.

41. Bach´s attitude towards Pietism must have been ambivalent. On the one hand, he would not have sympathized with Pietists´ strictures against elaborate church music. On the other, he did set many Pietist texts, and that convincingly and movingly, and possessed a goodly number of standard books by prominent Pietists. See eds. B. Schwendowius and W. Domling, Johann Sebastian Bach: Life, Times, Influence, (New Haven; 1984), pp. 27-9.

42. Leo Schrade, "Bach: The Conflict between the Sacred and the Secular," Journal of the History of Ideas 7 (2):168.

43. Edwards, Religious Affections, p. 256.

44. Jonathan Edwards, The Nature of True Virtue (Ann Arbor; 1960), pp. 6-8.

45. Edwards, Religious Affections, p. 106.

46. Herz, "Essays", p. 177.

47. I am indebted to Jan Wojcik, my colleague at Clarkson University, for suggesting this line of thought as well as making other invaluable suggestions for improving this chapter.

9

Bach the Architect: Some Remarks on Structure and Pacing in Selected *Praeludia*

Charles M. Joseph

In 1485, two hundred years before Bach's birth, the celebrated Renaissance designer Leone Battista Alberti defined the business of architecture as "appointing to the edifice and all its parts an appropriate place, exact proportion, suitable disposition and harmonious order, in such a way that the form should be entirely implicit in the conception."(1) My remarks stem from my interest in exploring certain structural relationships in Bach's music, particularly as they pertain to the concepts of proportion, disposition, and order of which Alberti speaks.

I have chosen for discussion several selected keyboard Praeludia that were initially written for the 1720 Klavierbuchlein fur Wilhelm Friedemann Bach, but by 1722 had made their way into their more recognizable form as Praeludia in the first volume of the Well-Tempered Clavier. A comparison of the original and final version, ostensibly at least, may prove revealing in terms of tracing how various compositional choices unfolded during the evolution of the work.

One should be aware of the specific challenge encountered by Bach in contemplating the design of the Praeludia. These are freely composed works that are not bound to any particular formal prescription such as might be the case in a stylized dance. More importantly, the Klavier-büchlein Praeludia (of which there are eleven), were written with a specific didactic goal--the improvement of keyboard technique for Bach's then nine-year-old son. Thus, these are genuinely functional works, conceived to present an obstacle to be overcome by the performer. Architecturally, this is of interest since any self-respecting architect worth his or her salt pertinaciously hangs to the dictum that any architectural design must present and solve a particular functional problem in an aesthetically creative fashion before the work may be deemed successful. As Joseph Esherick in Architects on Architecture (1966) proclaims, "Beauty is a consequential thing, a product of solving problems correctly."(2) While we may find such a pronouncement a bit austere, I think that a comparative study of the "Praeludia" from Klavierbüchlein to WTC will reveal that Bach in this instance indeed solved his problem most beautifully.

Before presenting four representative examples of these revisions, I should like to clarify my frequent allusions to my references to architecture. In raising the conjunction of music and architecture, I am aware that I may be opening a Pandora's box from which may fly a clutter of meaningless metaphors. Of course music and architecture have long provided a popular analogy--an analogy poetically portrayed by Johann Goethe's euphonious epithet of architecture defined as "frozen music." However, such a beguiling sentiment notwithstanding, one must be prudent in conjuring up commonalities between these two nonrepresentational art forms. Nonetheless, to preclude wholesale exploring what linguists refer to as "deeper grammatical relationships" would seem to be dangerously myopic, and in this sense I respectfully submit that at a tercentennial distance, perhaps our historical perception of Bach's "global impact," to borrow a phrase, may just be too restrictive and too parochial. If we are to eventually grasp the full significance of Bach's creativity, then I believe we should at least make some attempt at hypothesizing how Bach's structural designs transcend the boundaries of music literature and enter into the more broadly conceived universe of Alberti's architectual proportion, disposition and harmonious order.

Turning now to a comparison of the two versions of the Praeludia, a few apparent questions arise: (1) Why were the works altered at all? Do we from the luxury of hindsight sense any structural inadequacies? (2) How does Bach unify the original idea with the material revised--for the revisions are precisely that--re-visions, rather than freshly composed new works. (3) Can we detect any emerging structural patterns? (4) Finally, since we cannot ascribe purpose to Bach's emendations, can we contemplate how these alterations influence our thinking about the revisions? How do these changes affect our perception of the work, especially regarding the temporal dimension, that is, the actual pacing of musical events? The concept of pacing in music is surely as crucial as any spatial problem confronted by the architect. As Leonard Meyer suggests, "There are elusive forces shaping any rich human experience. Pace and timing (i.e. how long a particular sort of event continues, and how different sorts of events follow one another) are of central importance in music."(3) Finally, at the risk of giving away the punch line a bit prematurely, the totality of Bach's revisions seems in one way or another to effect the perceptual result of altering our temporal sense of how each work's architectural pacing flows.

Example 9.1 provides a congruence summary of the modifications made during the revisional process of the well-known Praeludium in C Major. The highest of the three staff systems (the one carrying the A, B, C brackets above) exhibits the draft of the 1720 WFB Klavierbüchlein as compared with the WTC version given in the lowest staff system. The middle system either lists those measures that remained constant during the revisional process, or briefly describes the changes listed directly above or below. Time does not allow a tracing of the numerous voice-leading alterations, but these constitute more localized event changes rather than significantly structural ones. What is informative is the deleted Klavierbüchlein bar seen under bracket A (originally m. 12) and the temporally compensatory bar added as the third measure notated above braket B of the lowest staff system. Thus, while there is an internal adjustment, the larger progression to the V7/IV in meter 20--notated in the middle system--consumes the same overall amount of time. A more critical change articulated at a strategic juncture in the macroformal architectual pacing is seen in bracket C. Immediately after, there is evident a reconceived cadential gesture. Obvious, too, is the extension of this section by seven measures as seen above bracket D. However, it would be capricious to dismiss this interpolation as one of mere elaboration. Rather, the newly voiced F-sharp to A-flat chromatic inflection in the bass of bracket C engenders a recasting of the subsequent cadential progression. It is indeed a causal inflection. Perceptually, we are dealing with architectonic layers of structure--inextricably interrelated, or as Heinrich Schenker suggests, our musical perception is formed by the connection and integration of levels of structure. While the F-sharp to A-flat revoicing enhances the arrival of the V chord (the last chord notated under bracket C in the middle system), as a structural consequence, this newly embellished dominant now demands greater temporal attention itself, precisely because of its newly gained architectual prominence. To borrow a common architectural analogy, the F-sharp and A-flat altered the V chord's structural environment, consequently affecting the tension, resolution, and structural balance--all of which collectively shape our perception of the overall design.

In thinking of this revision, the concept of rhythmicity, as coined by Alfred Korzybski in his book Science and Sanity, comes to mind. (4) As you know, architects are keenly aware of their designs in terms of visual rhythms since spatially such an aspect of structural pacing is one of the first to become apparent to the observer. Indeed, psychology places the stimulus of rhythm and "periodicity" in terms of its "evocativity" as only second to our olfactory sense. Patterns, accents, and meter are all constituent parts of architectural proportions as perceived in either aural or visual design. Regarding the temporal proportions in the Praeludium in C Major, the revisions observed obviously realign the internal architectural rhythm at every level. One notes, for example, that the interpolation of our previously discussed F-sharp to A-flat alteration occurs at the architecturally significant moment of .62 of the compositon's overall time span. While it is not my intention to argue for the regularity of golden sections in Bach's music (admittedly an interesting architectural study in itself), I must mention that, indeed, the revisions engineered throughout the Klaviebüchlein collection en route to the WTC without exception formally reshape the architectural pacing in closer conformance to the Fibonacci theorem so ubiquitous in the architectural reflections and designs of Alberti, Andrea Palladio, Charles-Edouard Le Corbusier, and, for that matter, even Pythagoras with his mystical pentagram.

Example 9.2 offers a section of the equally well-known Praeludium in C Minor--found next in order in both the Klavierbüchlein and WTC. As with the Praeludium in C Major, this work is similarly expanded, in this instance from 27 to 38 measures. Similar, too, is the rentention of the large initial section of this étude. The final five measures of the Klavierbüchlein score are given at the bottom of Example 9.2. Measures 23 and 24 continue the momentum that characterizes this study, while measures 25 through 27 exhibit a dominant-based cadence within a less active textural setting. Shown above this section is a portion of the WTC final version. The arrow from measure 23 to the corresponding bar below indicates the sameness of the music to this point; and, indeed, measures 24 and 25 are also identical. It is with measure 26 that the alterations commence. There is no need to belabor the obvious: during the revisonal process, Bach greatly expanded this close, whereas originally the cadence was reached more expediently. Here again, however, as with the previous example, one notes a similarly constructed interpolation rather than a simple appendage. The same pattern emerges: the V chord first appearing in bar 21 (as seen in the WTC score) now endures durationally for a substantially longer time span before its resolution. Indeed, the newly written Presto section (internally unified with the previous material through its motivic development) in itself continues its own fortification of the dominant function. Moreover, one observes the eventual resolution of the V chord in meter 34, not on the long expected tonic, but rather deceptively to yet another V7/IV function at the Adagio and regarding the revisional process more broadly for a moment, this V to V7/IV progression at meter 34 corresponds directly to the revision seen earlier during the course of the seven-measure extension in the Praeludium in C major under bracket D. Example, 9.3 summarizes the fact that not only is the progression itself identical, it is also structurally relatable. Finally, if I again may be permitted to generalize across the collection of these revisions, this kind of revisional pacing within the restructuring of the cadential gesture is quite common and obviously has the perceptual result of heightening the listeners' tension by prolonging the harmonic ambiguity a bit further.

Two final points must be briefly summarized: First: with the WTC measure marked Allegro (bar 35), we witness a return to the original material seen at bar 26 of the Klavierbüchlein--and I have drawn an arrow in Example 9.2 to clarify this reprise. However, even at this late stage of the work's pacing, Bach elects to once more expand the gesture vis-a-vis two more measures--namely: bars 36-37--thereby creating a linearly descending gesture towards the tonic's arrival. Second: a simliar architectural proportion in terms of the macroformal pacing is evident as a result of the entire thirteen-measure interpolation, for if we return to measure 25 of both versions, the point where the actual revisions begin, we can note a structural juncture of .63 of the final version's overall time line.

As a third example, consider a brief section from the Praeludia in D Minor and Major. Here the work is expanded through adding a new section rather than by interpolation. The D Minor is lengthened by eleven measures and the D Major by thirteen--a rather usual length of extension throughout the collection. Just as one might expect, Bach unifies the new with the old by developing the original figuration. Furthermore, the emphasis on slowing the perpetual-motion character of these two etudes by slowing the harmonic rhythm is employed as a means of achieving a less architecturally abrupt cadence. Examples 9.4a-b and 9.5a-b offer both versions of each work respectively. The reconstitution of the cadence through the use of extended diminished triads is evident. Again, the point of expansion in each arrives at a similar proportional juncture to the works previously mentioned. What we experience perceptually, I believe, is what architects refer to as sequence--a term employed in a slightly differing way from the musical usage of the same word. Architectually, sequence addresses the flow of time in that whatever comes later is shaped by what comes before. In the cadential constructions examined in this third example, as in the previous examples, to have continued the same seminal gesture (in every case a relentlessly propulsive motive because of its étude-like character) would have produced a rather unbalanced sense of time, without shape, and without the beginning, climax, and compensation that the architect Eugene Raskin speaks of as being fundamental to nearly any life process.

As a final example held to be representative of the revisional process, consider the Praeludium in E Minor--a thorough study of which would reveal the most dramatic changes in the entire collection. The work is expanded from 23 to 41 measures. Let us begin again with a brief look at the final cadence as illustrated in Examples 9.6a-b. The Klavierbüchlein version displays the same type of architecturally "unprepared" cadence as just discussed. The revision is given in Example 9.6b. I have reproduced here not only the cadence itself but the beginning of the newly composed Presto as well. Whereas in the earlier version Bach reached the cadence in meter 23, the later score reveals a reshaping of the same material toward the creating of a transitional passage. I remember a composition teacher telling me once that if I wanted to discover the true virtues of a well-formed work, I should carefully examine the seams. Architects speak of the same notion when discussing the problem of the "corner," a problem that seems to have occupied the Florentine architect Filippo Brunelleschi, who solved the problem by extending pilasters in a rhythmically ordered sequence around the corner. Returning to Example 9.6a, several perceptually clear changes are apparent: the right-hand flourish and subsequent resolution to the treble pedal E, as seen in the first two measures of Example 9.6b; the descending bass line (here I have circled the notes) that replaces the stationary E of the original (as I have circled in 9.6a); and finally, the extension of the same figuration as a motivic basis for the new Presto section. All seems to flow smoothly.

Three further and final observations follow: (1) Within the new

Presto section, the linear descent of the bass (and again I have circled the notes in 9.6b) arrives on the dominant pedal pitch B--the last measure of the score, which I have flagged with an asterisk. The pedal B continues until the final cadence (not shown here), but structurally interesting is the fact that the B when first reached marks a juncture of .63 of the expanded Presto section. (2) This same linear descent characterizes the old as well as the new section. Thus, its integration throughout the work as the fundamental organizational agent clearly brings a perceivable coherence across the transitional seam. (3) More speculative in its implication, the primacy of this descending bass gesture as the essential means of architectual unification seems to be replicated as the basic pitch material for the subsequent fugue subject (See Example, 9.7), thus inviting a study of even larger structural relationships. This is not to suggest that there was a premeditated effort to integrate Praeludium and Fugue--as some Bach scholars have contended--but rather to acknowledge the possibility of some common etymological derivative that we can comprehend subliminally through what the aesthetic morphologist refers to as "organic apperception," the subconscious understanding of the growth process.

This last point brings me to some concluding thoughts regarding our knowledge of Bach's own interest in this whole business of structural pacing. The fact is, there is little to suggest that Bach was consciously preoccupied with matters of architecture or proportional templates. Some scholars point to Bach's membership in Lorenz Christoph Mizler's Society of Musical Sciences as an indication of his theoretical interests, but his participation in that circle was at best lukewarm. There is no evidence to suggest that he was particularly enamoured by Jean-Philippe Rameau's theories, let alone aware of such grander structural treatises as Issac Newton's 1687 Mathematical Principles of Natural Philosophy in which the fundamental principles of motion are addressed--principles that coincidentally find their compositional analogue in much of the revisional work discussed here. Furthermore, as you are no doubt aware, there is a veritable federation of disciples who will argue cogently for Bach's immersion in the mysticism of numerology, whereby certain arithmetic sums, when decoded, can unlock the secrets of Bach's compositional logic.

Be that as it may, if there is a source of structural inspiration, perhaps it can best be traced most directly to Bach's genuinely fervent devotion to the theological tenets of Martin Luther, which, among other beliefs, included the adoption of the medieval doctrine of musica theorica,--a widely based philosophy that spoke of the perfect cosmos, rationally ordered by God according to measure and number. It is from this point, perhaps, that we can more safely gain access into Bach's conception of structural order at every dimension of the organic whole.

In raising this issue, I do not wish to construe any direct correlation between a few keyboard pieces and a rationally ordered universe. Conversely, I do submit that our approach to structural order in Bach might be extended to at least entertain a broader perspective in which we begin to examine order in Bach with the idea of architectural order in general. I find myself in agreement with Alfred Korzybski who comments that "if we want to understand anything at all, we must look for structure, relations, and ultimately, multi-dimensional order." (5) Certainly the notion of multi-dimensional order, architecturally speaking, is comparable to Schenker's Schichten--that is, levels of structure--and who more than Schenker relies on metaphor as a means of extrapolation in viewing music as part of his universal cosmos. Perhaps we should turn to disciplines beyond music to aid us in our structural studies. General semantics offers us the concept of referents whereby we may more precisely define our ideas of pacing, levels, balance, and so on as we construct abstraction ladders that eventually, one hopes, will lead to a clearer focus on true commonalities between discrete areas of inquiry. Perhaps we should pursue more tenaciously the connection between structural levels in Bach, as discussed by Schenker and others, with those recursions, isomorphisms, labyrinths and strange loops of which Douglas R. Hofstadter writes so eloquently.

I have found that through such a study as this I am personally able to gain a sharper understanding of a least some of the questions that may have met Bach as he went about revising the pacing of certain works. A simple comparative analysis of such revisions provides a fairly tangible glimpse into what appears to have been his concern with the overall compositional architecture. However, such opportunities for comparison are relatively rare, and at best provide only a brief window on the much larger issue of structural order. If we are to expand that window, then perhaps it is through metaphor and a broader approach to structural analysis that we can gain further insight into Bach´s genius and better grasp the architectural significance of his compositional order--an order that surely sweeps beyond the narrow boundaries of music.

NOTES

1.   See L. B. Alberti, De Re Aedificatoria (Florence: 1485); tr. Bartolo and Leoni as Ten Books on Architecture, Book 10 repr; (London: 1726); ed. J. Rykwert (London: 1965).

2.   Joseph Esherick,   Architects on Architecture, New Directions in America ed. P. Heyer (New York;   1966), p. 113.

3.   Leonard Meyer, Explaining Music   (Berkeley: University of California Press, 1978), p. 5.

4.   Alfred Korzybski, Science and Sanity (New York: The International Non-Aristotelian Library, 1933), p. 26.

5.   Ibid., p. 54.

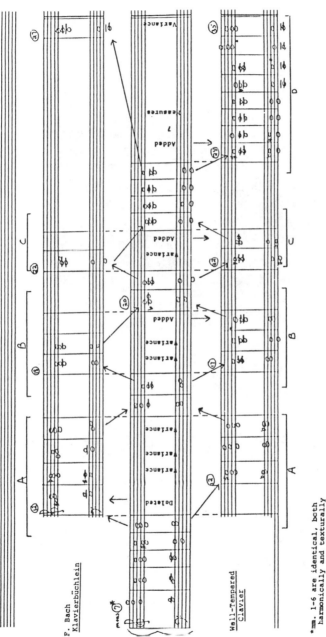

Example 9.1

W.F. Bach
Klavierbüchlein

Well-Tempered
Clavier

*mm. 1-6 are identical, both
harmonically and texturally

90   Charles M. Joseph

Example 9.2

WTC

Klavierbüchlein

Example 9.3

<u>WTC</u>, <u>Praeludium in C Major</u>

Extension   V--------------V7/IV ----------I Cadence

m.28   m.32   m.35

                              !

<u>WTC</u>, Praeludium in C Minor

                              ¦

Extension   V--------------V7/IV----------I Cadence

m. 26   m.34   m.38

Example, 9.4a
<u>Klavierbüchlein</u>,
D minor

Example, 9.4b
<u>WTC</u>, D minor

Example, 9.5a
Klavierbüchlein, D Major

Example, 9.5b
WTC, D Major

Example, 9.6a
Klavierbüchlein, E Minor

Example, 9.6b
WTC, E Minor

Example, 9.7
WTC, Fugue Subject, E Minor

10

Musical Expression and Musical Rhetoric in the Keyboard Works of J. S. Bach

David Schulenberg

In the nineteenth century both musicologists and performers took it for granted that the music of the past, when considered or performed at all, could be interpreted through customary approaches to such things as criticism and performance practice. This has changed, of course, with the efforts of modern musicologists and performers to reconstruct the interpretive traditions of the past. Naive assumptions and assertions about the expressive aspects of early music have been replaced by historical research into such things as the Figuren-and Affektenlehren. Modern performances based on the re-creation of historical instruments and performing practices have brought about considerable changes in how we perceive and experience early music, including its expressive qualities.

Thus, most thoughtful listeners, on hearing a harpsichord work of Bachs, understand that its expressive qualities are of a different nature from, say, the wit and drama of the Classical style or the atmospheric and programmatic evocations of Romantic music. Even so, most of our assumptions about later Baroque expression depend on modern discussions, such as that of Manfred Bukofzer, whose main point of reference is vocal music. (1) Of course, it is reasonable to assume a certain degree of likeness in the expressive modes of vocal and instrumental works, and those who have considered expressive aspects of Bach's keyboard music, in particular the organ compositions, have assumed that devices familiar from the vocal works, such as musical symbolism, are present there as well. This discussion will explore the possibilities and limitations involved in the similar procedure of applying the doctrine of musical rhetoric to Bach's keyboard music.

It has been suggested that the historical study of rhetoric is more than merely ancillary to understanding Baroque aesthetics and practice; it can serve as a window into the very system of thought itself that governed both education and serious thought and criticism during Bach's lifetime. (2) Even so, while rhetoric and the old humanistic educational system of which it was a part continued to influence the manner in which Bach and his contemporaries set texts to music or organized their musical treatises, in interpreting the music--any of it, vocal as well as instrumental--we must continually ask what exactly the study of musical rhetoric can teach us. We also must be wary of forming our own systems which, though conceived as attempts to make sense out of the theory and practice of the Baroque, may turn out to be little more than the embodiments of our own fantasies about the spirit of the past.

Thus, Peter Williams has argued against certain vague or flimsy notions about Bach's use of numerical or other symbolism, and has questioned whether we really learn anything by transferring the labels of rhetorical figures to procedures in real music. (3) His arguments suggest that musical rhetoric, while an important expressive element in Bach's early vocal music and perhaps some vocally inspired keyboard works, becomes less central as his style matures and encompasses new stylistic elements within an increasingly self-sufficient formal architecture. Musical rhetoric, moreover, may be of primarily biographical significance, telling us something about how a Baroque composer such as Bach thought about what he was doing, perhaps even something about his sources of inspiration. But it is not clear if this sort of information is of more than historical value.

The question might be approached by first defining exactly what is meant by "musical rhetoric," and then considering the relationship between expression and rhetoric in a few early and late keyboard works of Bach. Musical rhetoric as discussed by modern writers has meant things as distinct as the rules of counterpoint as set forth by Heinrich Schütz's student Christoph Bernhard and the Cartesian theory of the affects as applied to music by Johann Mattheson. (4) Naturally, both Bernhard and Mattheson adopt customary rhetorical lines of thought, among which is a penchant for the application of Greek and Latin terms to particular musical procedures, which they term figures by analogy to those of rhetoric. Yet, until Mattheson and other 18th-century writers actually tried to draw up a systematic theory of music modeled specifically on that of rhetoric and borrowing much of its terminology, the explicit relationship between music and rhetoric would seem to have been limited to one part of a composer's work: the setting of texts.

Thus, while both Bernhard and the young Johann Gottfried Walther, in his Praecepta der musicalischen Composition of 1707, (5) explain counterpoint by means of what could be called figures, Walther mentions only in passing the possibility that a composer might actually put into use some of the genuinely rhetorical fugues. Walther's Praecepta, incidentally, are highly retrospective, they are essentially a collection of notes on and abstracts from some of the most important German musical writings of the 17th century, and are probably more important in prefiguring the scholarly zeal and thoroughness that Walther was to show in his Musicalishes Lexikon of 1732 than for any direct relationship to J. S. Bach. Neither Bernhard nor Walther gives even a suggestion that rhetorical principles as such have anything to do with instrumental music. For the young Bach, "musical rhetoric," if he ever heard of it, would have consisted of properly setting a text to music: the art of conveying through music all the nuances and inflections that a trained orator would have conveyed through the spoken voice. Naturally, this art included an understanding of the various artifices of counterpoint, but the specifically rhetorical part of composition would have been confined to the rules and techniques of setting a text in the declamatory style still used in most German vocal music of the early 18th century. Bach himself is said to have known well the principles of musical rhetoric, but this may mean only that he, like all the better Baroque composers, was concerned with such things as correct declamation, particularly in recitative. (6)

It is at the beginning of his career that rhetoric, in this sense, seems to be the primary interest in Bach's music. (7) The early cantatas at times show an exaggerated impulse to display the figural artifice—contrapuntal as well as rhetorical—with which the older treatises are concerned. In addition, the young Bach employs certain distinctive musical ideas in these cantatas which are rhetorical in the sense that they represent responses to problems of declamation posed by the texts which he is setting. These devices go beyond simple types of musical symbolism or the use of stereotyped melodic figures; rather, they involve types of musical syntax whose origin presumably lay in the goal of setting the text as expressively as possible, which for a Baroque composer meant in a rhetorical manner in the best sense of the word. When we find similar types of musical syntax in more or less contemporaneous keyboard works, we have some basis for considering the extension of musical rhetoric into Bach's early instrumental music.

Indeed the fundamental musical style of both the early vocal and the early instrumental works might be described as rhetorical. Of course, the same is true of much of the instrumental music of the early and middle Baroque; what is notable here is the intensive use of certain rhetorical devices in the music of the young Bach, and in most cases the great technical skill with which they are handled.   Thus, some of the early works open with a highly self-conscious setting-out of a Thema or Inventio--what we would call a motive--which is articulated by expressive pauses and emphasized by immediate repetition, the latter being one of the fundamental rhetorical figures as well having an obvious and close parallel in both vocal and instrumental music. Rhetoric in this sense is characteristic of the type of fugue subject that is sometimes termed "repercussive," in reference to its iterations either of single notes or of larger units. (8) To be sure, such subjects occur not only in Bach's own early works but in the music of his North-German predecessors Johann Adam Reinken and Georg Böhm.   Bach's repercussive subjects, however, actually contain several distinct themata sharply etched by rests, which add to the rhetorical quality of the subject, although the latter is consequently quite different from the subjects of Bach's later instrumental fugues.

Example 1. a   Fugue in E Minor, BWV 533/2, first two entries
           b   Toccata in C Minor, BWV 911, first two entries
           c   Well-Tempered Clavier, Book 2 Fugue in G
               Minor, BWV 885/2, first two entries

Ex. 1a

Ex. 1b

Ex. 1c

Such subjects, even if admitting of stretto or other types of advan-
ced contrapuntal work, are more suited for fugues in which the focus is
on the material itself, not its treatment. Hence the abandonment of such
subjects in Bach's later keyboard fugues; a rare exception is the Fugue
in G Minor from the second book of The Well-Tempered Clavier (Ex. 1c),
which, if it was indeed composed as late as the compilation of the volume
suggests, is unusual also in its retention of a formal scheme not based
on modulation to successive tonal centers.

Simple repetition--the principle underlying "repercussion"--is the
basis of some more sophisticated devices which are still in some sense
rhetorical. For instance, a number of choral partite in ritornello form,
such as BWV 767/2 and 770/9, introduce a device reminiscent of the so-
called Divisen-Arie, in which fragments of the chorale melody are presented as mottos prior to the full statement of each phrase.

Example   2.   O Gott, du frommer Gott, BWV 767:
               Partita II, mm. 1-8

Another manifestation of rhetorical repetition is the obstinate re-
iteration of a single unvaried figure through a series of changing harmonies. It is found in the Sonata in A Minor from Reinken's Hortus musicus,
which Bach transcribed for harpsichord.   The idea occurs four times in
different movements, each time as part of a cadential pattern that seems
to be derived from the early Baroque conceit of avoiding the resolution
of a dissonance--the fourth (a") over the final E in the bass--for
expressive purposes. The same device occurs also in several variations
of the Aria variata, BWV 989, an early work particularly close to the
North-German organ tradition. Something very similar occurs in a few of
George Frideric Handel's early works, suggesting that both composers
might have picked it up during their days in or around Hamburg. The two
works illustrated in Example, 10.3 also employ the variation principle
especially cultivated in the suites of Reinken, Dietrich Buxtehude, and
other Northern composers of the middle Baroque.

Example, 3 a.   Sonata (after Reinken), BWV 965: Presto,
                end

        3 b.   Handel, Suite in D Minor, HWV 437,
                Corrant, mm. 23-28

Example 3a

Ex. 3b

        The device in Example, 10.3 is to be distinguished from a more
familiar sort of repetition in which transpositions of the same arpeg-
giated motive compose out a long series of different harmonies, as in the
opening Prelude of The Well-Tempered Clavier.   Though neither form of
repetition is directly analogous to anything in Bach's vocal works, the
latter type seems to have a parallel in Baroque poetry.   Such arpeggiation, described by the theorist Friedrich Erhard Niedt, occurs in
toccatas by Reinken and Bohm which were probably familiar to Bach; the
latter, characteristically, employed it with both greater imagination and
greater persistence in a number of well-known works.(9) Perhaps the most
extraordinary instance is in a section of the early Praeludium BWV 922,
which, though labelled Fuga in one source and written in a quasi-
imitative texture, is in essence an arpeggiando passage containing no
less than ninety-one statements of the principal motive. (10)   Such
writing seems to be a musical parallel of the poetic device found in the
text of the alto arioso of BWV 72, and in the Litany of BWV 18, both by
the Weimar court poet Salomo Franck, in which a long series of lines is
written as a series of variations on the same formula. (11) The success
of the device depends on the writer's ability to maintain a growing sense
of surprise or wonder at the increasing cleverness or brilliance in the
variations of the formula, creating a gradual swelling of tension which,
at least in the musical versions of the device, must be very carefully
nurtured and sustained by the performer.
        A few of Bach's early instrumental works make intensive use of
motives that can be understood as rhetorical in a semantic, not a merely
syntactic, way.   Most important is the employment of half-steps in a
manner that corresponds to that of the early cantatas, where the contrapuntal texture of several movements is permeated with both chromatic and
diatonic half-steps in response to a pathetic text or, more precisely,

one of intense supplication.   This motive should probably not be
identified with the so-called sigh motives of later music, which often
are little more than a stylistic mannerism.   In these early works of
Bach, the half-step may be reinforced by such things as the minor mode
and chromatic, even Frescobaldian, voice-leading; it is repeated with an
almost obsessive insistence in several movements of the early Cantata BWV
131 as well as in some more or less contemporary keyboard pieces.

Example 4. Aus der Tiefe rufe ich, Herr, zu dir, BWV 131:

a.   opening chorus mm. 85-89
b.   bass aria, mm. 1-6 (oboe, solo bass, and continuo parts)

Example, 4a

Example, 4b

Yet, while the motive in BWV 131 seems to be associated with such textual ideas as Sünde zurechnen and die Stimme meines Flehens, it would seem wrong to extend any specific meaning to keyboard works in which the motive similarly pervades the texture. Even in the vocal works, the use of the motive probably does not constitute text painting or musical representation as such; like many musical symbols, it achieves its expressive effect simply by signaling that the music is of a type routinely associated with highly affective texts. What sets Bach apart is that, even in his youth, he already seeks to deepen the expressive element by referring simultaneously to several different genres. In BWV 131, the pathetic associations of the half-step motive are juxtaposed against those of the chorale melody introduced in the course of the bass aria.

The same motive is woven into the texture of two early but very different
keyboard works, the one-movement Sonata in A Minor, BWV 967, and the
"Lamento" from the famous Capriccio sopra la lontananza del suo fratello
dilettissimo, BWV 992. (12)
     It is hardly necessary to describe the latter piece except to point
out that half-steps permeate both parts through the conventional chromatic descent in the ostinato bass and the half-step motives and mitation
of the bass in the treble. The sonata is less familiar, but perhaps provides a more exact parallel to the cantata in the rhetorical repetitions
of the half-step ideas. These occur in a recurring passage, functioning
somewhat like a ritornello theme, which is first heard in m. 5, following
the introduction to this unjustly neglected little piece.

     Example, 5. a. Capriccio, BWV 992: Lamento, mm. 1-9
                  b. Sonata, BWV 967, mm. 1-13, 20-5

Ex. 5 a

Ex. 5 b

Ex. 5 b

Both movements, especially through their occasional use of figured bass, suggest their close relationship to non-keyboard genres. The vocal reference made in the "Lamento" becomes explicit in a third piece, the "Aria" in the Praeludium et Partita, BWV 822, which employs figured bass in its ritornellos. The title aria is often found attached to 17th-century instrumental pieces, although many of them are arias in the archaic sense of being composed on a ground bass, like the "Aria" of the Goldberg Variations. But the imitation of vocal genres--and thus of musical rhetoric--is quite clear in the movements from the Capriccio and Partita. It is of particular value for criticism because it gives some idea of Bach's expressive aspirations in his youthful keyboard music. In these pieces he is not merely striving to depict a narrative, as Johann Kuhnau had done; the effort to render the keyboard instrument expressive leads to rhetorical, and thus quasi-vocal, keyboard writing, possibly several years before the composition of any actual vocal works. The tradition of writing instrumental recitative in the Chromatic Fantasy and in works by Bach's sons thus has antecedents in early works by Sebastian Bach that imitate vocal idioms of the late 17th century. At the same time, Bach's use of fugue as the culminating number in the early Capriccio as well as in the later Chromatic Fantasy and Fugue suggests an effort to frame the rhetorical or programmatic ideas within a more abstract exposition of contrapuntal skill and keyboard dexterity.

Though the Chromatic Fantasy and other relatively late keyboard works may occasionally make a direct imitation of vocal genres or rhetorical devices, it is difficult to find instances of explicit musical representation; there is no enigmatic meaning hidden within the recitative section of the Chromatic Fantasy, for example. More important, Bach places the imitation of rhetoric within an increasingly elaborate abstract framework. To be sure, certain 18th-century writers extended semantic principles to instrumental music, and by the end of the century it was taken for granted that instrumental music not only could represent affects, but could depict concrete objects. Thus Bach's son Carl Philipp Emanuel was confronted by no less than two exegetical texts added by the poet Heinrich Wilhelm von Gerstenberg to the fantasia that concludes the set of sonatas published in conjunction with Bach's Versuch über die wahre Art das Clavier zu spielen. (13) Such efforts depended on certain commonly acknowledged types of association, such as those on which Mattheson drew for his list associating the commonly used keys with certain affects. But the attempt to find objective meaning in instrumental music--that is, to draw an over-literal analogy to rhetoric--is quite distinct from the project of describing the art of composition as a purely formal parallel to the art of constructing an elegant and persuasive verbal argument.

At least some eighteenth--century writers recognized a distinction between representational figures--Johann Adolph Scheibe's musicalische Metaphora (14)--and those that were of purely musical significance, motives, as we would call them. Friedrich Wilhelm Marpurg reminded his readers that "in the stricter sense one understands by the term Figuren the use of the figures of composition for a certain affect or subject Gegenstand, and these are referred to by certain terms taken from rhetoric." (15) The "figures of composition" of which Marpurg speaks are the abstract motives that the North German theorists of the 18th century recognized as arising through the composing out of harmonies-what Johann Philipp Kirnberger and others traced to the realization of an abstract figured bass line. (16)

Indeed, perhaps the greatest value of rhetoric as applied to late Baroque instrumental music lies not in the occasional analogy that can be drawn to the figures and topics, but rather in the fundamental insight, provided by rhetorical thought, that music can be understood as a concatenation of distinct particles or figures. Seventeenth-century

position treatises such as Bernhard´s do include individual motives among
the musical figures--indeed, ornamentation treatises from as early as the
16th century follow this line of thinking--but only with the 18th-century
writers are these types of figures clearly distinguished from others of a
non-motivic nature.   A related innovation of the 18th century was a
systematic approach to the articulation of stereotyped motives in the
performance of instrumental music. Individual figures--that is, motives--
apparently were meant to be clearly articulated from each other; moreover, certain figures, such as the various species of arpeggiation
enumerated by Quantz in his book on flute playing, or the types of
figures whose bowings are illustrated in string treatises, possess a
stylized internal type of articulation that gives each figure a distinctive rhythmic shape.

Peter Williams has recently made some specific suggestions regarding
keyboard articulation and rhetoric, but few of them are supported by the
sources. (17)   For example, the slurs that he suggest for chromatic
scales, extending even over bar lines, have few precedents before
Wolfgang Amadeus Mozart.   Those slurs that are actually written into
Bach´s keyboard music generally correspond exactly with what a string
player would play in one bow, that is, they represent a particular type
of motive characterized by the absence of any internal articulation.   It
seems doubtful that most figurae-by which Williams seems to mean both
rhetorical figures and motives at different points-can be characterized
simply in terms of either a legato or a detached touch.   Most of the
motives whose articulation patterns are illustrated in string and woodwind sources, and which figure prominently in Bach´s keyboard music,
involve intricate combinations of slurs and subtly distinct varieties of
detached notes--especially the latter--and probably minute rhythmic
nuances as well.   A sensitive keyboard player will be wary of trusting
the "natural articulations" which certain motives may suggest, and will
instead bear in mind the prescriptions of contemporary instrumental
treatises as well as Bach´s own indications in instrumental works, giving
each gesture a character and individuality of its own without, of course,
destroying the continuity of the larger line in which the figures occur.

This approach to articulation, made possible by the particular construction of the music, may be the only audible element that can be
described as rhetorical in much of Bach´s later keyboard writing, where
direct imitations of vocal music are rare and palpably rhetorical effects
are less the focus of attention than the contrapuntal artifice, the
written-out embellishment, or the formal architecture.   As with other
aspects of style, the rhetorical articulation of Bach´s mature keyboard
music represents not a departure from but rather an intensified version
of the general practice of the time, enriched by a diverse and often
surprising profusion of striking ideas.   For example, the "Sarabande"
opens with a series of disjunct gestures of greatly varying character and
rhythm.   Yet the traditional Sarabande rhythm remains intact in the
underlying harmonic rhythm which these gestures embellish.

Example 6.   Partita IV, BWV 828:   Sarabande, mm. 1-3

The player's duty in conveying the rhetoric of the piece consists in differentiating these gestures: making clear the impetuosity of the opening Schleifer, the sudden languor of the following Pralltriller (a favorite ornament of the Berlin style), and then the odd stasis in the following measure. Bach's technique here is an individualistic synthesis of the current Italian manner of embellishment with some French overtones. It is highly rhetorical, albeit in a strictly metaphorical sense, and is a far cry from the more literally rhetorical Schütz style occasionally imitated in Bach's earlier keyboard music.

This being the case, what can we conclude about the relationship of rhetoric to expression in Bach's later keyboard works? Surely we would all agree that this "Sarabande" is expressive music, even though we cannot write a text for it or draw easy analogies between it and any of Bach's Leipzig vocal works. Bukofzer's influential article posited that Baroque music employs what he called an "iconic" or "allegorical" mode of expression in which discrete musical entities serve as signs for specific things or ideas, including affects. Perhaps this is true insofar as the musical signs themselves are usually small figures corresponding to the most minuscule articulations in the work's rhythmic scheme—concise motives that fit neatly into carefully articulated melodic lines. Bukofzer supposed that the Baroque use of "iconic" signs distinguished it from later music in which expression was communicated intuitively, "without the mediation of the intellect" as he put it. Modern semioticians might find this formulation a little crude; the chief distinction between Baroque and later expression may be that in what Bukofzer termed musical allegory the signs are small figures in the surface, while in later music the signs take the form of larger music processes, such as the extended crescendo or the prolonged dissonance. In a vocal setting a Baroque composer typically focuses on a single significant word in the text, representing it through a single characteristic motive. We might designate such a mode of expression, dependent on small musical figures, as rhetorical, recognizing, however, that in so doing we merely draw a parallel between the forms, not the content, if any, of music and rhetoric. Diverging from the rhetorical mode of expression, later composers attempted to evoke a general mood or atmosphere, an approach first clear in the music of Christoph Willibald Gluck and other members of his generation, though not his North-German contemporaries or the older sons of Bach.

It seems unlikely, however, that Bukofzer's theory of iconic or allegorical figures or signs could be applied in Bach's keyboard music, except in the very limited number of explicitly programmatic pieces, such as the Aria di Postiglione in the early Capriccio. The use of certain figures may, of course, tell us that a piece belongs to a particular genre. But, especially with Bach, we should be wary of assigning works mechanically to genres, such as the varieties of fugues listed by Johann Gottfried Walther.   It is highly arbitrary to classify the fugues of The Well-Tempered Clavier, for example, into rigid categories when one of Bach's prime aims in his later instrumental music seems to have been to incorporate galant dance rhythms or melodies in popular style into imposing contrapuntal edifices. (18) Bach freely mixes musical ideas associated with contrasting genres; one can readily cite, for example, highly chromatic themes in Bach's later music that cannot be understood as pathetic, among them the counter subject of the Fugue in A-flat from the second book of The Well-Tempered Clavier.

Example 7. Well-Tempered Clavier, Book 27:
          Fugue in A-flat, BWV 886/2, mm. 1-4

Example 7.

Similar considerations would apply to categories based on other musical elements, such as key.

While Bach's mature vocal settings continue to employ word painting and musical rhetoric in the strict sense, even in the vocal music it is probably a mistake to suppose that these are the only or even the principal modes of expression. For what we call the expression in any mature work of Bach's can hardly be confined to the musical surface. The failure to recognize the heirarchic nature of musical structure and its relevance to musical expression--particularly in 18th-century music, with its complex tonal and rhythmic heirarchies--is a limitation that Bukofzer's discussion of Baroque expression shares with many treatments of musical expression in general. Especially in Bach's later work, the imitation of rhetoric is subsumed into structures in which detail is subsidiary to the larger design. In the vocal works the adoption of textual and musical forms derived from late-Baroque Italian opera leaves musical rhetoric predominant only in the recitatives. Elsewhere, musical rhetoric in the strict sense will explain little more than occasional mannerisms in the melodic line.

Bach's adoption of tonally organized ritornello designs and related heirarchic forms during his Weimar years thus was linked with a decline in the priority assigned to the imitation of rhetoric in the instrumental music. In the process Bach abandoned a certain charm that his early keyboard works share with many of their seventeenth-century German models. Also cast aside, however, was the danger of stiffness and even pedantry-- empty rhetoric in the modern sense, such as threatens to take hold in the repetitious Fuga of BWV 922. Of course, Scheibe and others criticized even the mature Bach for persisting in Baroque turgidness and obscurity. Writing on Bach's sacred vocal works, Scheibe drew an explicit analogy between Bach and the seventeenth century master of exaggerated poetic rhetoric Johann Caspar von Lohenstein.(19) While we can now perceive the subordination in Bach's Leipzig works of rhetorical artifice to larger concerns, Scheibe's point is not entirely mistaken, for Bach's style often juxtaposes an exceptional variety of single motivic figures or a seemingly contradictory set of references to diverse genres.

The ideal of Mattheson and other eighteenth century writers on expression was a naturalness supposedly absent from the old style; the latter was characterized not only by its polyphonic complexity but by the qualities of its rhetoric, as Scheibe's comment about Lohenstein suggests. The other side of the naturalness favored by the eighteenth century writers was rationalism, which was manifested in their reference for symmetrical, clearly articulated architectural forms, and in their efforts to produce a consistent, scientific Affektenlehre. Particularly in his formal architecture, Bach seems to have followed the tendencies of his contemporaries. Although he did, in some of the latest keyboard works, make considerable use of the stile antico, Bach rarely if ever returned to the episodic, declamatory, even irrational manner of his own early keyboard music. The Chromatic Fantasy, though probably not originating from the Leipzig years, is thus something of an anomaly among Bach's mature keyboard compositions, for otherwise neither Bach nor his sons seem to have had much inclination to write down their free fantasias, in which the direct imitation of rhetoric seems to have played a

particularly important role. In written compositions Sebastian Bach preferred to incorporate the relatively arbitrary, improvisational surface
of the free style within a fairly rationalistic architecture, while
Friedemann and Emanuel Bach held off writing down their improvisions
until their old age, with a few exceptions. Formally stylized sonatas
make up the great bulk of their written keyboard music.

Critics like Scheibe who could not see beneath Sebastian Bach's
often intricate musical surfaces regarded them as a mark of his continuing adherence to an old and obsolete system of musical thought and expression. Curiously enough, Johann Abraham Birnbaum's defense of Bach--
even if deriving its ideas from the composer himself--is somewhat feeble
and ponderous, rhetorical in the bad modern sense. But an a Magister of
rhetoric at Leipzig, Birnbaum was primarily an instructor of lawyers and
preachers, and one might therefore allow for a certain old-fashioned pon-
derosity in his style. We have no way of knowing how Bach felt about
extended speculations on the relation of music to rhetoric, but we must
not forget that the game of seeing a musical form such as fugue as a
complex metaphor for rhetoric was itself an exercise in a peculiarly
Baroque mode of thought, even if it engaged Mattheson and other fashionable eighteenth century writers. The doctrine of musical rhetoric is far
from irrelevant to Bach's keyboard music. It may even play a necessary
part in any theory of musical expression in that repertory. But, like
any metaphor, musical rhetoric will play a role which is more that of
suggestion than of explanation or analysis.

NOTES

1. Especially see Manfred Bukofzer; "Allegory in Baroque Music,"
Journal of the Warburg and Cortauld Institutes 3 (1939-1940); 1-22.

2. See, for example, George Beulow, "Music, Rhetoric, and the Concept of the Affections: A Selective Bibliography," Music Library Association Notes 30; No. 2 (1973); 250-51.

3. In addition to comments in Peter Williams' The Organ Music of
J. S. Bach 3 vols., Cambridge: Cambridge University Press, 1980-1984,
especially vol. 3; pp. 65-91, see his "The Snares and Delusions of Musical Rhetoric: Some Examples from Rent Writings on J. S. Bach," in Alte
Musik/Praxis und Reflexion, ed. Peter Reidmeister and Veronika Gutmann
(Winterthur: Amadeus, 1983), pp. 230-240. One need look no further than
several other articles in this Festschrift for the 50th anniversary of
the Basel Schola Cantorum to find examples of writers caught in the
snares discussed by Williams.

4. Bernhard's composition treatises, "The Treatises of Christoph
Bernhard," are translated by Walter Hisle, in The Music Forum 3 (1973);
pp. 31-79. For a sympathetic summary of Mattheson's aesthetics, drawn
primarily from his Volkommene Capellmeister (Hamburg, 1739), see Peter
Kivy, The Corded Shell: Reflections on Musical Expression (Princeton:
University Press, 1980), pp. 39-45.

5. Peter Benary in Jenaer Beiträge zur Musikforschung, ed. Heinrich
Besseler (Leipzig: VEB Breitkopf und Hartel, 1955).

6. In the famous defense of Bach's music delivered in 1738 by Johann Abraham Birnbaum, reprinted in Bach-Dokumente, Band II, Fremdschriftliche und gedruckte Dokumente zur Lebensgeschichte Johann Sebastian
Bachs 1685-1750, ed. Werner Neumann and Hans-Joachim Schulze (Kassel:

Bärenreiter, 1969), entry 409; pp. 296-97; trans. in Hans T. David and Arthur Mendel, The Bach Reader, rev. ed. (New York: Norton, 1966), pp. 239-47.

7. Peter Williams points out that only in the early vocal works does Bach appear to imitate the idiom of Schutz; see pp. 234-35 of Williams, "Snares and Delusions."

8. See, for example, Christoph Wolff´s article on Bach in The New Grove Dictionary of Music and Musicians, ed. Stanley Sadie vol. 1 (London: Macmillan, 1980), p. 813.

9. Niedt illustrates the arpeggiation of a series of harmonies in Chapter 6 of the second volume of his Musicalische Handleitung (Hamburg, 1706) (unpaginated); compare Reinken´s Toccata in G (in Corpus of Early Keyboard Music, ed. Willi Apel; Vol. 16, 1967) and the final section of the Prelude, Fugue and Postlude of Böhm in (Sämtliche Werke, ed. Johannes Wolgast, Wiesbaden: Breitkopf und Härtel, 1952-1963). The Reinken work is in the so-called Andreas-Bach-Buch, and the other is in the Mollerschen Handschrift, both of which are closely associated with the young Bach.

10. Although the work-list in The New Grove considers the work "doubtful," it is difficult to understand who but the young Bach could have composed this remarkable, if not wholly balanced, piece. The rubric Fuga comes from the copy by J. T. Krebs, Berlin, Deutsche Staatsbibliothek, Mus. ms. Bach p. 803, which also gives the title of the piece as Fantasia; see Hermann Zietz Quellenkritische Untersuchungen an den Bach Handschriften pp. 801-3, (Hamburg: Wagner, 1969), p. 65.

11. This Baroque poetical device is pointed out by James Day in The Literary Background to Bach´s Cantatas (New York: Dover, 1961), pp. 37-38.

12. There apparently is no concrete evidence for the recurring suggestion that BWV 967 is the arrangement of a movement from an ensemble work. In any case, its style seems consistent with that of other equally well-authenticated original works by the young Bach.

13. On Gerstenberg´s additions see E. Eugene Helm, "The ´Hamlet´ Fantasy and the Literary Element in C. P. E. Bach´s Music," The Musical Quarterly, 58, (1972); 281-82. Emanuel Bach himself used the conventional language which described a composer as a Maler; see the quotation given by Gottfried Ephraim Lessing and cited by Max Schneider in his edition of two Telemann cantatas, in Denkmäler der deutscher Tonkunst 28 (Leipzig, 1908), fn. lvi.

14. Johan Adolph Scheibe, Critischer Musicus. Neue vermehrte und verbesserte Auflage (Leipzig, 1745), pp. 646-48.

15. Anleitung zum Clavierspielen. Zweyte verbesserte Auflage (Berlin, 1765; facs. rpt., New York: Broude, 1969), p. 39. Marpurg made a further distinction between what he called figures of composition and figures of performance, the latter consisting primarily of ornaments such as trills and mordents. Earlier Baroque writers had occasionally referred to certain embellishments of either sort as figures, but had not clearly distinguished them from other sorts of musico-rhetorical figures.

16. See my "Composition as Variation: Inquiries into the Compositional Procedures of the Bach Circle of Composers," Current Musicology 33

(1982); pp. 57-87.

17. Peter Williams "Figurae in the Keyboard Works of Scarlatti, Handel and Bach: An Introduction," in Bach, Handel, Scarlatti/ Tercentenary Essays, ed. Peter Williams (Cambridge: Cambridge University Press, 1985), pp. 327-46.

18. Johann Gottfried Walther´s Lexicon, (Musicalisches Lexicon, 1732) pp. 432-34, lists terms for various genres of fugue which are the basis of Stefan Kunze, "Gattungen der Fuge in Bach´s Wohltemperiertem Klavier," in Bach-Interpretation, ed. Martin Geck (Gottingen: Vandenhoeck und Ruprecht, 1969), pp. 74-93.

19. The relevant passage is translated in David and Mendel; Bach Reader, p. 238.

Work on this article was supported in part by a Mellon Fellowship held at New York University during 1984-5, for which I am most grateful. I am also grateful to the editor for permitting me to mention here two items that have come to my attention since this article was written: Robert Hill, in his dissertation   "The Möller Transcript and the Andreas Bach Book: Two Keyboard Anthologies from the Circle of the Young Johann Sebastian Bach" (Harvard University, 1987), pp. 364-6, 448-58, points out that the text of BWV 967 as given in Ex. 10.5b (especially measures 6-7) is partly conjectural, while confirming that the piece (whose authenticity has been questioned) is an original keyboard work of J. S. Bach. Wolfgang Wiemer (following earlier suggestions by Peter Schleuning) has argued for a quasi-programmatic interpretion of the Chromatic Fantasia; see "Carl Philipp Emanuel Bachs Fantasie in c-Moll--ein Lamento auf den Tod des Vaters?" Bach Jahrbuch, 74 (1988), 166.   I discuss this in an article forthcoming in Journal of Musicology.

11

The Original Circumstances in the Performance of Bach's Leipzig Church Cantatas, *"wegen seiner Sonn- und Festtägigen Amts-Verrichtungen"*

Don L. Smithers

There are several perplexing aspects to the problem of understanding precisely how and where Bach performed his Leipzig cantatas. Many questions are, of course, concerned with original Aufführungspraxis-- with the how of performing Bach´s concerted church music. But there is another difficulty: that of knowing where and under what circumstances Bach performed his Kirchenstücke for the principal Sundays and feast days of the Lutheran church year.

It is generally assumed that Bach´s church cantatas were performed in St. Thomas´s church. Bach was, after all, the "Cantor zu St: Thomae," but he was also the "Director Chori Musici Lipsiensis," a title that he used in the subscript to many official documents during his Leipzig Amt. Furthermore, the second of the fourteen "Puncten" contained in the "Endgültiger Revers des Thomaskantors,"(1) which Bach had to agree to and sign before assuming his duties, was the condition that "Die Music in beyden Haupt-Kirchen dieser Stadt, nach meinem besten Vermögen, in gutes Aufnehmen bringen..."(2) This meant that Bach´s responsibilities were not restricted solely to St. Thomas´s church; that his concerted vocal music proper to the principal Sundays and feast days of the church year was also heard elsewhere, namely in the other Leipzig Hauptkirche of St. Nicolai.

The long-held assumption that the usual place of performance for Bach´s Leipzig church cantatas was St. Thomas´s church is, therefore, historically incorrect.(3) It was, in fact, at St. Nicolai that as many if not more of the performances of Bach´s concerted church compositions were heard. St. Nicolai was the church used for Leipzig academic convocations and such occasions for public worship as the annual celebration of the Ratswahl Gottesdienst on the last Monday of every August.(4) Consequently, all of Bach´s Ratswahl cantatas were performed there, and not in the St. Thomaskirche. Moreover, the annual performance of the Passion music on Good Friday was given alternatively from year to year in St. Thomas and St. Nicolai. However, there were numerous other times when Bach´s Kirchenstücke were performed in St. Nicolai, and under his own direction. For it comes as even a greater surprise to those inured to thinking of St. Thomas´s church as the normal location in which Bach performed his Leipzig church catatas when it is learned that the feast day works were, in fact, performed twice the same day and in both principal churches of the city. But surprise if incredulity notwithstanding, the evidence for this is both various and incontrovertible.

When, for example, Bach wrote to the Saxon Elector and King of Poland on December 31, 1725, explaining why he could not personally supervise the music in the University Church, he said:

daß der Cantor zu St: Thomae wegen seiner Sonn- und Festtägigen Amts-Verrichtungen Keinesweges in Stande sey, auch zug-
leich das Directorium der Music in der Universitäts-Kirche
ohne Praejudiz und Unordnung übernehmen, immaßen er fast zu
eben der Zeit in der Kirchen zu St: Thomae und St: Nicolai
die Music zu dirigiren hätte...(5)

In the same document (and in the same context) he added that, while the
organist of each church must stay in his place to the end of the service,

dahingegen der Cantor nach verrichteter Music herausgehen
kann, und den Kirchen-Liedern biß zum Beschluß des Gottesdienst eben nicht beywohnen darff, gestalt auch der selige
Kuhnau zu seiner Zeit beydes [i.e., in both Hauptkirchen]ganz
wohl ohne Praejudiz and Confusion verwaltet hat...(6)

If, in fact, Bach had to be in two places at almost the same time,
as he says his predecessor Kuhnau had before him, it is logical to ask
why--to what end, or for what purpose? A definitive answer is to be
found in the appropriate surviving word books (libretti) that were published for the advantage of those desirous of better understanding the
texts to the respective cantatas (or other texted works) for the various
Sundays and/or church festivals for which the music had been composed.
Some of these text books were published for all of the "Cantaten auf die
Sonn= und Fest=Tage durch das gantze Jahr";(7) others were published for
individual and specific occasions, such as the Texte zur Music,/ so nach
gehaltener/ Raths=Wahl=Predigt/ in der/ Kirche zu St. Nicolai/ von dem/
Choro Musico abgesungen worden./ Leipzig 1749; (8) or, more to the point,
for an individual series of works proper to a particular season, such as
the ORATORIUM, Welches/ Die heilige Weyhnacht/ über/ In beyden/ Haupt=
Kirchen/ zu Leipzig/ musiciret wurde./ Anno 1734.(9) The superscriptions
with each of the appropriate texts to the six parts of Bach´s Weihnachts
Oratorium (BWV 248I-VI), indicate the places and times of performance.
They indicate in no uncertain terms that some parts were performed twice
the same day (see Table 11.1).

T 11.1

Times and Places for the Performance(s) of Each Part of
Bach´s Weihnachts Oratorium in 1734/35

BWV 248^I "Am Isten Heil. Weyhnacht=/Feyertage,/ Frühe zu
St. Nicolai und Nachmit=/ tage zu St. Thomae."

BWV 248^{II} "Am 2. Heil. Weyhnachts=/Feyertage./ Frühe zu St.
Thomae. Nachmittage/ zu St. Nicolai."

BWV 248^{III} "Am. 3. Heil. Weyhnachts=/Feyertage./ Zu St.
Nicolai."

BWV 248^{IV} "Aufs Fest der Beschneidung/ Christi [i.e. 1st
January, New Year´s Day, which is the Feast of the
Circumcision] / Frühe zu St. Thomae; Nachmittage/
zu St. Nicolai."

BWV 248^V "Am Sonntage nach dem/ Neuen Jahr./ In der Kirche
zu St. Nicolai."

BWV 248^{VI} "Am Feste der Offenbahrung/ Christi [i.e. Drei
Könige, or Feast of the Epiphany] . /Frühe zu St.
Thomae. Nachmittag/ zu St. Nicolai."

It is clear that parts one, two, four, and six of Bach´s Weihnachts
Oratorium were, in fact, performed on Saturday, Christmas Day, Dec. 25,
1734; Sunday, Dec. 26, 1734; Saturday, January 1, 1735; and Thursday,

the Feast of the Epiphany, January 6, 1735, respectively. On each of
these days the appropriate part of the work was given twice: in the morning and again in the afternoon (presumably at Vespers), alternatively in
the churches of St. Nicolai and St. Thomas. Only parts three and five
were given once: on Monday morning, December 27, 1734 and on Sunday morning, January 2, 1735. It should be noted, moreover, that they were given
in the church of St. Nicolai, not that of St. Thomas.

The reason why parts three and five were performed only once on each
occasion is not readily apparent. Perhaps in the Lutheran tradition the
third day of each of the High Feasts (Christmas, Easter, and Pentecost)
was not accorded the same liturgical importance as the first and second
days. It is to be noted in the appropriate word books that only the
first and second days of the three High Feasts required the principal
music to be performed in both churches, while the third day's music was
always given a single performance in St. Nicolai. The contemporary
sacristan of St. Thomas's church, Johann Christoph Rost, recorded in his
Nachricht (10)   that "Den 3. Feiertag ist frühe zu St. Thomas keine
Music, d. nur zu St. Nicolai." There were, of course, musical propria
heard in the St. Thomaskirche. What Rost and others meant by Music was
concerted music for voices and instruments (the so-called Figural=Musik).
As Günther Stiller noted, "denn unter "Music" und "musiciren" im Gottesdienst wurde in jener Zeit immer die Darbietung einer von obligaten
Instrumenten begleiten Figuralmusik verstanden." (11) That part five was
given only once is explained by the fact that the day of the performance
was an ordinary Sunday and not a feast day.

From various evidence it is clear that double performances of Bach's
concerted church music on the same day were not an anomaly limited merely
to performances of the Weihnachts Oratorium. A tabulation of the few
surviving text books gives some indication of the particular days on
which Bach had to conduct his Leipzig cantatas in double performances at
the two principal churches of the city (see Table 11.2). We may infer
that the surviving text books do, in fact, represent a paucity of the
actual number of such books published during the eighteenth century.
Stiller, for example, remarked that Leipzig cantata text books had been
printed from the time of Johann Kuhnau's Amt and throughout the entire
eighteenth century. (12) What is to be learned from these lamentably few
surviving books, however, should in no way be construed as somehow exceptional. The years for which there is no such surviving evidence were
most likely the same liturgically as any other year. We assume, therefore, that the same conditions and regulations existed during those
periods for which there are no known text books.

T 11.2

Single and double performances of Bach's Leipzig cantatas as
Noted from the Surviving Text Books for the Following Years.

1724(13)

Sun. 16 Jan.	BWV 155	"Am andern Sonntage nach der/ Erscheinung Christi./ In der Kirche zu St. Thomae."
Sun. 23 Jan.	BWV 73	"Am dritten Sonntage nach der/ Erscheinung Christi./ In der Kirche zu St. Nicolai."
Sun. 30 Jan.	BWV 81	Am vierdten Sonntag nach der/ Erscheinung Christi./ In der Kirche zu St. Thomae."

Wed. 2 Feb.	BWV 83	"Am Fest der Reinigung Mariä./ Früh in der Kirche zu St. Nicolai und in der Vesper/ zu St. Thomae."
Sun. 6 Feb.	BWV 144	"Am Sonntage Septuages[imae]./ In der Kirche zu St. Thomae."
Sun. 13 Feb.	BWV 181	"Am Sonntage Septuages[imae]./ In der Kirche zu St. Nicolai."
Sun. 20 Feb.	BWV 22	"Am Sonnt[age]. Quinquages[imae]. oder Esto Mihi./ In der Kirche zu St. Thom[ae]."
Sat. 25 March	No known setting: music probably by Bach. (14)	"Am Fest der Verkündigung Mariä./ Früh in der Kirche zu St. Thomae und in / der Vesper zu St. Nicolai."

The text for the first movement (presumably for chorus) is from the Prophet Isaiah, Chap. 7, verse 14: "Siehe, eine Jungfrau ist schwanger und wird einen Sohn gebähren, den wird sie heissen Immanuel."

1724(15)

Sun. 9 April	BWV 31	"Auf den ersten Heil[igen]. Oster=Tag. / Frühe in der Kirche zu St. Nicolai, und in der Vesper/ zu St. Thomä."
Mon. 10 April	BWV 66	"Auf den andern Heiligen Oster=/ Tag./ Frühe in der Kirche zu St. Thomä, und in der Vesper/ In der Kirche zu St. Nicolai."
Tues. 11 April	BWV 134	"Auf den dritten Heiligen Oster=/ Tag./ In der Kirche zu St. Nicolai."
Sun. 16 April	BWV 67	"Am Sonntage Quasimodogeniti./ In der Kirche zu St. Thomä."
Sun. 23 April	BWV 104	"Am Sonntage Misericordias/ Domini./ In der Kirche zu St. Nicolai."

1725(16)

Sun. 17 June	BWV 177	"Dominic[a] III. post Trinitat[is]./ Zu St. Nicolai."
Sun. 24 June	Text only: music probably by Bach.	"Festo St. Johannis./ Früh zu St. Thomä, nachmittag zu St. Nicol[ai]."

The text to the first movement (presumably for chorus) is taken from the Gospel of St. Luke, Chap.1, verse 68, the "Lobgesang des Zacharias": "Gelobet sey der Herr, der Gott Israel, denn er hat besucht und erlöst sein Volck."

| Sun. | 1 July | Text only: music probably by Bach. | "Dominica V. post Trinitat[is]./ Zu St. Nicolai." |

The text to the first movement (presumably for chorus) is an abbreviated paraphrase of Proverbs 10, 22: "Der Seegen des Herrn machet reich ohne Mühe."

| Mon. | 2 July | Text only: music probably by Bach. | "Festo Visit[ationis]. Maria./ Früh zu St. Thomä, nachmittag zu St. Nicol[ai]" |

The text to the first movement (for chorus), which is repeated at the conclusion of the work (according to the direction following the last line of printed text, "Chorus repetatur ab initio"), is the first line from Martin Luther's translation of the Magnificat (Luke, Chap. 1, verse 46ff.): "Meine Seele erhebt den Herrn, und mein Geist freuet sich Gottes meines Heylandes."

| Sun. | 8 July | Text only: music probably by Bach. | "Dominica VI. post Trinit[tatis]./ Zu St. Nicolai." |

The text to the first movement appears to be a conflationary paraphrase of several scriptural passages from the fifth Book of Moses (Deut. Chap. 32, verse 35ff.), the Sermon on the Mount. (Matt. Chap. 6, verse 12ff.), and St. Paul's Letter to the Romans (12:19): "Wer sich rächet, an dem wird sich der Herr wieder rächen, und wird ihn auch seine Sünde behalten. Vergieb deinem Nechsten, was er dir zu leide gethan hat, und bitte denn, so werden dir deine Sünden auch vergeben."

1731(17)

Sun.	25 March	BWV	31	"Am ersten/ Heiligen Oster=Tage/ frühe zu S. Nicolai, Nachmittags/ zu S. Thomae."
Mon.	26 March	BWV	66	"Am andern/ Heiligen Oster=Tage/ frühe zu S. Thomae, Nachmittags/ zu S. Nicolai."
Tues.	27 March	BWV	134	"Am dritten/ Heiligen Oster=Tage/ in der Kirche zu S. Nicolai."
Sun.	1 April	BWV	42	"Am Sonntage Quasimondo-/ geniti./ In der Kirche zu S. Thomae."
Sun.	8 April	BWV	112	"Am Sonntage Misericor-/ dias. /In der Kirche zu S. Nicolai."

1731(18)

Sun.	13 May	BWV 172	"Am ersten/ H eiligen . Pfingst=Feyertage./ Frühe zu St. Nicolai, Nachmittags zu/ St. Thomae."
Mon.	14 May	BWV 173	"Am andern /H eiligen . Pfingst=Feyertage./ Frühe zu St. Thomae, Nachmittags/ zu St. Nicolai."
Tues.	15 May	BWV 184	"Am dritten/ H eiligen . Pfingst=Feyertage./ In der Kirche zu St. Nicolai."
Sun.	20 May	BWV 194	"Am Fest=Tage der H. Heil./ Dreyfaltigkeit. [Trinity Sunday]/ Frühe zu St. Thomae, Nachmittags/ zu St. Nicolai."

The alternation of performances of the Leipzig Hauptgottesdienst Figuralmusik seems to be consistently from one church to the other based on the morning service, irrespective of where the second hearing of a double performance was on a particular Sunday or feast day for a Vesper service. The pattern of alternation from Easter Sunday morning to Trinity Sunday morning in 1731 (see above) is a reasonable paradigm, which, excepting any unexpected anomalies that might have been caused by breakdowns of organs, fires,(19) or other unknown circumstances, may serve as a basis for extrapolating in other years the place or places of performance from one Sunday and/or feast day morning to the next. This pattern is a traditional one and is mentioned by a number of contemporary Leipzig chroniclers and liturgists.(20)

The apparent inflexibility in the alternation of services from one church to the other is, of course, to be noted in the rigid sequence of annual performances for the Good Friday passion music. Supposedly begun by Kuhnau in 1721 with a "Musicirte Passion" sung at St. Thomas's church "am CharFreytag in der vesper,"(21) the strict alternation of the passion music from one church to the other persisted well after Bach's arrival. Even in 1724, after the word book had already gone to press with its title having indicated that the passion music was to be given once again in St. Thomas (on account of Bach's stated need for more space and his complaint that the Nicolai church's harpsichord was in a state of disrepair,(22) the Senatus of Leipzig ordered the performance to take place in St. Nicolai anyway, with any additional expenses incurred by Bach's musical requirements to be paid for by the town council.

There are profound musical and logistical implications of Bach's large-scale Leipzig liturgical compositions having been performed in relatively quick succession at one church and then the other on the principal Sundays and holy days for which they were written. The fact that large works such as the sixth part of the Weihnachts Oratorium (BWV 248VI), cantata BWV 31 (Der Himmel lacht), and numerous others -- many that are not accounted for in the all-too-few surviving word books, but that must be presumed to have been performed in accordance with the same customs, e.g. the high feast day music of the Himmelfahrts-Oratorium (BWV 11), cantata BWV 147, and the Oster-Oratorium (BWV 249) were performed twice and in two different places, does raise several questions. Not the least of these are concerned with the performers, the need of getting from one church to the other, problems of fatigue for some performers with difficult parts having to sing or play the same music twice in

succession and in two different places, and the likelihood for mishap of
the Thomas Cantor, his choir and orchestra having to descend from one
choir gallery, exit into the streets, transverse the town from one side
to the other, enter the second church and ascend into another choir
gallery.(23)   The possible sights and sounds conjured up in one's imagination from all this implicit activity are as lively as they are interesting.

The implications of double performances raise in the first instance
the question of singers.   Was it only the erster Chor that performed
these works? We know from Bach's own testimony that he provided suitably
trained choirs of Thomanerschüler for four churches of Leipzig.   In 1729
he stated that there were three choirs of twelve voices each (3S, 3A,
3T, 3B) "In die Kirche zu S. Nicolai, Zu S. Thomae, [und] Zur neüen
Kirche."(24)   These were the first, second and third choirs respectively
(note that Bach associated his "erster Chor" with St. Nicolai). There
was a fourth choir of eight voices (2S, 2A, 2T, 2B), and this last choir,
as Bach says, "muß auch die Petri Kirche besorgen. etc."(25)   The total
number of trained singers from the Thomasschule at this time, therefore,
was forty-four; the total in all likelihood does not include the actual
number of Alumni St. Thomae, some of whom would not have been suitably
trained, or whose voices would no longer have been usable.   Furthermore,
some individuals may have been used as instrumentalists only.   In 1730
Bach stated in the official "Eingabe an der Rat der Stadt Leipzig" that
the total number of "Alumnorum Thomanae Scholae ist 55," and that these
were divided into four choirs.(26)   Moreover, he stated that the students
who sang in the choirs of St. Thomas, St. Nicolai, and the "Neüen Kirche"
must all be musical.   The smaller choir for the Peters-Kirche was less
so, having only to sing hymns and the like.

In another "Eingabe" written to the town council of Leipzig in 1736
(concerning his difficulties with the rector, Johann August Ernesti, over
the choice of choir prefects), Bach said that the "musicalischen Kirchen
Stücke" (cantatas) were mostly of his own composition (suggesting, as was
indeed the case, that the music of other composers was used from time to
time(27) and that these pieces were sung by the first choir and were
incomparably more difficult and complicated   ("ohngleich schwerer und
intricater") than the pieces sung by the second choir -- adding that this
was the case only on feast days ("zwar nur auf die FestTage musiciret
werden"). (28)   Another facet of this complex situation is revealed in
the rector Ernesti's "Eingabe" to the Leipzig town council on September
13, 1736, where he explained his own position in the quarrel with Bach
over the choice of choir prefects.   There he stated that the "ander Chor"
(second choir) was directed on feast days by the second prefect and that
Bach himself conducted the first choir (the first prefect at that time,
Maximilian Nagel, having played the violin).   What is not clear is what
the situation was on the principal Sundays and feast days with respect to
the singing of the other portions of the liturgy in the two churches of
St. Thomas and St. Nicolai.   Since the "muscialischen Kirchen Stücke"
were sung at both churches on these occasions, once in the morning
Hauptgottesdienst at one church and again in the vesper service at the
other, was there an Umtausch of both the first and second choirs from one
church to the other? -- or was there only a complimentary choir in each
church made up of the weaker singers who merely sang hymns, while the
first choir (possibly augmented by the best singers from the second and
third choirs) sang the more difficult music and then processed across
town to the other church for the repeated performance?   What the Leipzig
University professor of philosphy and town chronicler Christoph Ernst
Sicul (Sickel) noted in his Annales Lipsiensis for 1717 may provide one
or two clues to help answer this question:

Was die hohen Feste anbetrifft, so wird in beyden erwehnten
Haupt-Kirchen eine figural-Music vom gedachten Cantore veran-
staltet, also nemlich, daß die Principal-Music Vormittags, in
derjenigen Kirche, da der Herr Superintendens prediget, itzo
zu St. Nic olai . von ihm dem H err n.   Cantore Kuhnau at
that time selbst, in der andern Kirche aber, d.i. zu St.
Thomas, die Music von denen Thomas-Schülern bestellet wird,
dagegen Nachmittags die Haupt-Music zu St.Thomas vom Contore,
und die geringere zu St. Nicolai wiederum von einem Praefecto
Thomano dirigiret wird: worauf den andern Feyertag die Principal-Music früh zu St. Thomas, Nachmittags aber in der
Nicolai-Kirche, und also, wie Tages vorher, geweschselt wird
... in den beyden Haupt-Kirchen, da beydes die Figural- als
Choral-Music von dem Directorio des Cantoris Thomani depen-
diret, wird an gemeinen Sonntagen wechselsweise in der einen
Kirche figuraliter musiciret, in der andern aber nur Teutsche
Lieder chorales gesungen und die Orgel drein gespielet.(29)

It is not inconceivable that those who sang "nur Teutsche Lieder"
were but two on a part (if that), while some others who may have been
rather better singers and normally belonged to the second and third
choirs were added to the first. The one-time "Rektor der Thomasschule,"
Johann Matthias Geßner (or Gesner), did report in his edition of Quintilian's Institutio oratoria that Bach directed a choir and orchestra of
some thirty to forty musicians.(30)   No doubt the first choir and
orchestra were not always up to such strength, but it is hard to imagine
that the music for the three great church festivals was not peformed with
an augmented ensemble made up of the better singers from the other choirs
as well as intrumentalists from the university, the community at large,
and, in particular, the "Bachische Collegium Musicum."(31)   Bach himself
said in 1725 that the university "Studiosi, welche Liebhaber der Music,
sich allzeit gern und willig dabey finden laßen; So hat sich meinerseits
mit denen Studiosis einiges Unvernehmen niemahls ereignet, sie pflegen
auch die Vocal- und Instrumental-Music bey mir unverweigerlich und bis
diese Stunde gratis und ohne Entgeld zu bestellen."(32)
    Christoph Wolff has suggested an actual connection with Bach's
Collegium Musicum in the performance of such specific cantatas as BWV 174
and 29. (33)   The second is, of course, the often revived Ratswahl
cantata and, inasmuch as it was performed in the Nicolai Kirche with,
presumably, no services in the other churches to siphon off singers and/
or players, we must assume that Bach had a performing ensemble of rather
optimum numbers.   The scoring of cantata 119, also a Ratswahl composition, would indeed suggest that this particular annual event was one
for which the concerto was sung and played with a larger ensemble than
was usual. Wolff also mentioned that the performance of the Weihnachts
Oratorium was made possible only by virtue of the new "structure" of the
musical forces involving the Collegium Musicum. This may well have been
the case, inasmuch as the scoring of this work strongly urges us to
consider the size of ensemble that was not only intended but actually
used. As Wolff concluded,

The Collegium Musicum provided Bach with essential services
of his church performances, as we have seen, and certain special projects, such as the Christmas Oratorio of 1734-35, were
made possible only on the basis of this new structure. (34)

Certainly the performance of the Dramma per Musica overo Cantata gratula-
toria (BWV 215) and the other Huldigungsmusik heard earlier in the season
(35)   would have required the kind of forces as evidenced by Bach's
Leipzig Collegium Musicum for various performances, both in 1733 and

1734--notwithstanding the number of surviving instrumental and vocal parts.(36)

It is not certain how long the tradition of the concerted music for the high feast days at Leipzig being performed by the erster Chor persisted in the eighteenth century. There is some evidence that during Bach's Amt there was a need to rethink and reorder the established traditions whereby the second and third choirs had been required to sing elsewhere on the principal Sundays and holy days and to perform a less difficult musical fare than that performed by the first choir. The often quoted "Kurtzer, iedoch höchstnöthiger Entwurff" that Bach sent to the Leipzig Rat in August, 1730 suggests that the musical situation had deteriorated to some degree since the Thomas Cantor had taken office some seven years earlier.(37) Reading between the lines, there is a certain feeling that Bach's musical requirements were being frustrated by economic considerations, a falling enrollment of musically talented students in the Thomasschule, and a decline in the quality and availability of professional instrumentalists (Stadtpfeifer) from the Leipzig municipal orchestra. There is no doubt that Bach's stated optimum requirements for a "musicalischen Chor" of four sopranos and an equal number of altos, tenors, and basses were not being met, and that he seems to have had some difficulties even providing a trained choir of only three singers on a part. What the consequences were of Bach's "Entwurff" remains unknown. It is not unthinkable that some reduction had to be made in the size of the second and third choirs in order to maintain the necessary number and quality of singers in the first choir. That the second choir was eventually abolished for the musically demanding feast days is confirmed by an entry in Johann Christoph Rost's previously mentioned Nachricht. Sometime after Bach's death, Rost's chronicle made note of the following:

A[nn]o. [17]?? wurde die seither gewöhnliche doppelte Kirchen Music an den hohen und anderen Festen zu St. Thomas und St. Nicolai abgeschafft. Bis hierher war am 1. und anderen Festtag zu Ostern, Pfingsten und Weihnachten, desgleichen an jeden andern Festtage in beiden Kirchen Music... Auf geschehenen Vorstellung des Herrn Cantoris Doles aber... wurde vom hochlöbl ichen . Consistorio resolviret, die Music des anderen Chores abzuschaffen....(38)

The circumstances surrounding the performance of Bach's Leipzig Kirchenmusik are gradually coming into sharper focus. As traditional musical practices and local customs are better understood and verified by contemporary historical sources, the better will be our perception of the actual conditions under which Bach had to operate and the manner in which his concerted church compositions were performed. However, there are some very obvious and notable gaps in our present knowledge. One of these has to do with the relationship between the surviving performance material and the way in which the cantatas were rehearsed and subsequently performed. Some time ago Alfred Dürr pointed out a number of the anomalies and what appear to us today as incomprehensible if inexplicable contradictions with respect to the "original Auffürungsmaterial."(39) As Dürr said, "Die Folge davon ist, daß oft eine erschreckende Zahl von Kopierfehlern stehen bleibt, die bei der Aufführung keinesfalls (etwa aus dem Gedächtnis von den Proben her) auch nur in annähernder Zahl richtiggestellt werden konnten."(40) Moreover, as Dürr correctly observed, "Nicht minder aufschlußreich ist die Beobachtung dessen, was in den Originalstimmen Bachscher Kantaten nicht anzutreffen ist."(41) He then listed in three categories the kind of things that are missing, either entirely so "oder fast völlig"--the sort of things like musical accidentals, corrections, indications of tempo, solo versus tutti, articulation markings, dynamics, and many other details (not the least of which

are bar numbers) that leave one to wonder if many of the performing parts
were in fact ever used.   It is the errors of ommision that are particularly troubling in this respect.   For if a part has wrong notes it is
easy to understand how a competant musician could quickly make the necessary adjustments without necessarily leaving any markings.   But if a part
is missing notes or, worse, entire bars, rests, and the like, it is very
difficult to see how such a part could have been used in an actual performance without the necessary corrections, additions, etc., having been
made before hand.   To understand this serious anomaly may lead us toward
a better understanding, not only of Bach´s music in particular, but of an
entire musical process in general.   What may be gained thereby is a more
perfect knowledge of contemporary performance practices and a deeper
appreciation of Bach´s methods in preparing some of his most important
music, and under conditions which were not always propitious.

Appendix

The Lutheran Church Festivals
As Celebrated at Leipzig
During the Cantorship of
Johann Sebastian Bach

A.   The Three Great Feasts, each celebrated on three successive festival
days, each day having concerted vocal music performed by Bach´s erster
Chor and orchestra, the first two with repeat performances in the afternoon vesper service at one or the other Leipzig Hauptkirchen than that
for the morning Hauptgottesdienst (the first and third morning services
were always held in St. Nicolai): (42)

1. Christmas

A fixed feast, always on December 25 (and 26, 27)

Am ersten Heiligen Weyhnacht=Feyertag (25. xii.)
        Morning service (Hauptgottesdienst) St. Nicolai
        Afternoon service (vespers) St. Thomas

Am andern [2nd] Heiligen Weyhnachts=Feyertage (26. xii.)
        Morning service St. Thomas
        Afternoon St. Nicolai

Am dritten Heiligen Weyhnachts=Feyertage (27. xii.)
        Morning service only St. Nicolai

2. Easter

A moveable feast, but always on a Sunday, determined by
the first full (paschal) moon after the Spring equinox

Am ersten Heiligen Oster=Tage (Easter Sunday)
        Morning service St. Nicolai
        Afternoon service St. Thomas

Am andern Heiligen Oster=Tage (Easter Monday)
        Morning service St. Thomas
        Afternoon service St. Nicolai

Am dritten Heiligen Oster=Tage (Easter Tuesday)
        Morning service only St. Nicolai

3. Pentecost (Whitsuntide)

A moveable feast, the fiftieth day or seventh Sunday
after Easter

Am ersten Heiligen Pfingst=Feyertage (Whitsunday)
    Morning service St. Nicolai
    Afternoon service St. Thomas

Am andern Heiligen Pfingst=Feyertage (Whitmonday)
    Morning service St. Thomas
    Afternoon service St. Nicolai

Am dritten Heiligen Pfingst=Feyertage (Whit-Tuesday)
    Morning service St. Nicolai

B. The Ten Lesser Feasts, each with double performances of concerted vocal and instrumental music performed only on the day of the festival by the erster Chor in one and then the other (morning and afternoon) of the two Hauptkirchen of St. Thomas and St. Nicolai(43) (the church chosen for the morning service was, by a process of alternation, dependent upon the church where the previous morning service had been held):(44)

1. Fest der Beschneidung Christi (Feast of the Circumcision), New Year's Day, January 1.

2. Epiphanias (Epiphany) or Feste der Offenbahrung (or Erscheinung) Christi (sometimes referred to as Drei Könige Fest, i.e., Feast of the Three Kings -- the Magi), January 6.

3. Mariae Reinugung (Feast of the Purification of the Blessed Virgin), sometimes referred to as Lichtmeß (Candlemas), February 2.

4. Mariae Verkündigung (Feast of the Annunciation), March 25.

5. Himmelfahrt Christi (Ascension Day, or Holy Thursday), a moveable feast, being the fortieth day, or fifth Thursday, after Easter.

6. Trinitatis or Fest=Tage der H. Heil. Dreyfaltigkeit (Trinity Sunday), a moveable feast, being the next Sunday after Whitsunday (Pentecost).

7. Festo St. Johannis or Johannisfest (Feast of John the Baptist), June 24.

8. Festo Visitationis or Mariae Heimsuchung (Feast of the Vistation, commemorating the visit of the Blessed Virgin Mary to her cousin Elizabeth, who was pregnant with St. John the Baptist), July 2.

9. Michaelisfest (Feast of St. Michael the Archangel), September 29.

10. Reformationsfest (Reformation Day, commemorating the Protestant Reformation on the anniversary of the day when Martin Luther is reputed to have nailed to the door of the Schloßkirche at Wittenberg his ninety-five theses challenging the practice of indulgences), October 31.

NOTES

1.   Bach-Dokumente [hereafter referred to as BD], herausgegeben vom Bach-Archiv Leipzig...(3 vols., edited by Werner Neumann and Hans-Joachim Schulze, Leipzig, Basel, etc., 1963-1972: I, Schriftstücke von der Hand Johann Sebastian Bachs; II, Fremdschriftliche und gedruckte Dokumente zur Lebensgeschichte Johann Sebastian Bach 1685 - 1750; III, Dokumente zum Nachwirken   Johann Sebastian Bachs 1750 - 1800), vol. I, document   92, pp. 177-78.

2.   Ibid. p. 177 item 2.

3.   Many authors since Bach´s day have made note of this fact, including Philipp Spitta, Johann Sebastian Bach, Fünftes Buch 2, Leipzig 1930, p. 15; Charles Sandford Terry, Bach; a biography, Oxford 1962, pp. 160-1; and Arnold Schering, Musikgeschichte Leipzigs von 1723 - 1800 (vol. III in the three-vol. study by Wustmann and Schering), Leipzig 1941, p. 43.   Yet, as we shall see, none but the earliest have made it clear that on the principal Sundays and feast days Bach was obliged to take his erster Charles Sandford Terry, Bach; a biography, Oxford 1962, pp. 160-61.   Yet, as we shall see, none but the earliest have made it clear that on the principal Sundays and feast days Bach was obliged to take his erster Chor from one to the other Hauptkirchen for a repeat performance of the Figuralmusik.   A number of highly reputable and famous modern Bach scholars and performers, when approached with the preliminary facts in this matter, displayed a certain amount of incredulity if not scepticism.   Yet, most of the surviving facts that are now known support the original contention and verify Bach´s own statements.

4.   Strictly speaking, the date for the Ratswahl Gottesdienst was determined by the day on which the Feast of St. Bartholemew fell (August 24).   On the Sunday immediately preceding the feast day the Leipzig parishioners were informed from the church pulpits about the choice of the new town council. The official ceremonies and service of installation in St. Nicolai, however, were always held on the Monday immediately following St. Bartholomew´s Day, which, as it happens, was always the last Monday of the month.

5.   "The Cantor of St. Thomas´s, in light of his official Sunday and feast day obligations, was in no way in a position to take on also the direction of the music in the University Church without harm or disorder, inasmuch as at very nearly the same time he had to conduct the music in the churches of St. Thomas and St. Nicolai." (BD I; p. 34ff).

6.   "The Cantor on the contrary can leave after taking care of the music and is not needed to be present for the chorales at the end of the service, as was also the custom at the time of the late Kuhnau, who discharged his duties extremely well·in both [churches] without vexation or disorder." (BD I p. 35).

7.   From Picanders Ernst=Schertzhaffte und Satÿrische Gedichte, Dritter Theil, Leipzig... 1732, p. 79.   Facs. in Sämtliche von Johann Sebastian Bach vertonte Texte, ed. Werner Neumann.   Leipzig 1974, p. 326 ff.

8.   Facsimile in Neumann, p. 420.

9.   Facsimile in Neumann 1974, p. 448.

10. Johann Christoph Rost: Nachricht, Wie es, in der Kirchen zu St: Thom[ae]: alhier, mit dem Gottes Dienst, Jährlichen sowohl an Hohen Feste, als andern Tagen, pfleget gehalten zu werden, auffgezeichnet von Johann Christoph Rosten, Custode ad D. Thomae. anno 1716.   I am most grateful to Dr. Armin Schneiderheinze, Director of the Nationale Forschungs- und Gedenkstätten Johahn Sebastian Bach der DDR, for allowing me the privilege of studying a type-script of Rost's manuscript during one of my many visits to Leipzig.

11. Günther Stiller, Johann Sebastian Bach und das Leipziger gottesdienstliche Leben seiner Zeit, Kassel and Basel, 1970, p. 65.

12. Stiller 1970, p. 68.

13. Full title page: Texte/ Zur Leipziger/ Kirchen=Music,/ Auf den/ Andern, dritten, vierdten Sontage/ nach der Erscheinung Christi [Epiphany],/ Das/ Fest Mariä Reinigung,/ Und die Sonntage/ Septuagesimae, Sexagesimae,/ Esto mihi,/ Ingleichen/ Auf das Fest/ der Verkündigung Mariä,/ 1724./ Leipzig,/ Gedruckt bey Immanuel Tietzen.   See Neumann 1974, p. 422 ff.

14. There are several works accounted for in the text books for which there are no known musical settings.   It is more than likely that these were composed by Bach.   Alfred Dürr (Zur Chronologie der Leipziger Vokalwerke J. S. Bachs, Basel 1976) has used the expression "höchstwahrscheinlich von Bach" to settle the question of attribution.

15. Full title: Texte/ Zur Leipziger/ Kirchen=Music,/ Auf die/ H[eiligen]. Oster=Feyertage,/ Und die beyden folgenden/ Sonntage Quasimodogeniti/ und Misericordias Domini./ 1724./ Leipzig,/ Gedruckt bey Immanuel Tietzen. Sec Neumann 1974, p. 428 ff.

16. Full title page: Texte/ Zur Leipziger/ Kirchen=Music,/ Auf den/ Dritten Sontag nach Trinitatis,/ Das/ Fest Johanis des Täuffers,/ Ingleichen/ Den fünfften Sonntag/ Trinitatis,/ Das Fest der Heimsuchung Mariä,/ Und/ Den sechsten Sonntag Trinitatis,/ 1725./ Leipzig,/ Gedruckt bey Immanuel Tietzen. See Neumann 1974, p. 432 ff.

17. Full title of word book: Texte/ Zur Leipziger/ Kirchen=MUSIC,/ Auf das/ Heil[igen]. Oster=Fest,/ Und/ Die beyden/ Nachfolgenden Sonntage./ Anno 1731. See Neumann 1974, p. 438 ff.

18. Full title of word book: Texte/ Zur/ Leipziger/ Kirchen=MUSIC,/ Auf die/ Heiligen/ Pfingst=Feyertage,/ Und/ Das Fest/ Der/ H. H. Dreyfaltigkeit./ Anno 1731. See Neumann 1974, p. 444 ff.

19. The day to day historical record of events at Leipzig during the time of Bach's tenure is very imperfect.   One can anticipate just so far what life was really like on a daily basis without more precise knowledge of the many possible and unforseen mishaps or other unpredictable happenings which would have disturbed if not altered the normal course of events.   For the evening of March 6, 1726, for example, Johann Heinrich Zedler's Lexikon (vol. 16, 1737; "Leipzig," col. 1802) mentions the following:

Den 6. Mertz Abends im sechs Uhr enststund ein allgemeines Schrücken, indem auf dem Schüler-Chore in der Nicols-Kirche eine Flamme entstund, und eher zum Fenster heraus schlug, als man etwas darinne wahrgenommen hatte.   Die Gelegenheiten hierzu hatte ein Kohl Feuer gegeben, dessen sich die Instru-

mentisten bedient und unter einer Banck gesetzt hatten, da
denn hernach der Wind hinein geblasen und das Holz entzündet
hatte; doch ward es glücklich wieder gelöscht.

[Around six o´clock on the evening of March 6th there was a
terrible commotion when a fire broke out in the choir gallery
of the Nicolai church, and flames shot up at the windows before anyone inside knew what was happening. The circumstances
for this were caused by a charcoal heater, used by the instrumentalists, which had been placed under a bench and, being
fanned by a gust of wind, set fire to the wood near it.
Luckily, it was soon put out.]

March 6, 1726 was, incidently, Asche-Mittwoch (Ash-Wednesday)!

20. Stiller, Bach, pp. 40, 67.

21. See Rost, Nachricht...anno 1716, fol. 24r-v, and BD II, pp.
140-42.

22. See Johann Zacharias Trefurth´s "Verlegung" of April 3, 1724
in BD II, pp. 139-40 (English trans. in Bach Reader, p. 96).

23. Walking at a quick pace, the present author has gone several
times to and fro from St. Thomas´s church to the Nicolai Kirche, crossing
the center of Leipzig by various routes in an average time of approxi-
mately eight minutes.   One assumes that the entire erster Chor and orchestra during Bach´s time would have taken from between ten to fifteen
minutes to go from the one church choir gallery to the other.

24. BD I, pp. 60, 250.

25. BD I, p. 250.

26. BD I, p. 60.

27. It is now known that church compositions of Johann Ludwig Bach,
Kuhnau and others were performed while Bach was the Director Chori Musici
Lipsiensis.

28. BD I, p. 88.

29. From Christoph Ernst Sicul´s year book of 1717, Neo annalium
Lipsiensium Continatio II, p. 568 ff.:

"Concerning the High Feasts, there is for both the principal churches
mentioned a Figuralmusik provided by the aforesaid cantor, specifically
the Principalmusik [the cantata] from the cantor himself before noon in
that church where the superintendent preaches, at present St. Nicolai,
but in the other church, i.e., St. Thomas, the music is taken care of by
a student of the Thomasschule. On the other hand, the principal music in
the afternoon is once more conducted by the cantor at St. Thomas, while
the less important music is again directed by a prefect of the Thoman-
erchor at St. Nicolai. Whereupon on the second feast day the principal
music is given earlier at St. Thomas and in the afternoon at St. Nicolai,
and thus, like the day before, it is alternated. Inasmuch as both the
concerted music and that of the chorales depend on the direction of the
Thomascantor, on ordinary Sundays [for which the music is heard only once]
it is performed alternately [from one week to the next]; in one church
there is the concerted music, while in the other only German chorales are

sung in addition to organ playing."

30. M. FABII QVINCTILIANI DE INSTITVTIONE ORATORIA... PERPETVO COM-
MENTARIO ILLVSTRATI A IO. MATTHIA GESNERO, Göttingen 1738, p. 61: "...si
videre...Bachium, vt hoc potissimum vtar, quod meus non ita pridem in
Thomano Lipsiensi collega fuit: ...sed omnibus eundem intentum, & de xxx
vel xxxx adeo symphoniacis,... For a more complete text and translations,
see BD II, p. 331 and David and Mendel, The Bach Reader (1966), p. 231.

31. For a discussion of Bach having had augmented vocal and instru-
mental forces for the performance of the Figuralmusik on the principal
Sundays and holy days of the church year, see Don L. Smithers: "Abiding
Discrepancies between Historical Fact and Present-Day Practice in Perfor-
mances of Music by J. S. Bach," (Beiträge zur Bachforschung, vol. 2,
Leipzig 1982, pp. 36-45), and Hans-Joachim Schulze: "Johann Sebastian
Bach und Georg Gottfried Wagner - neue Dokumente" (Bach-Studien 5, Leip-
zig 1975, pp. 145-52), as well as the same author's "Studenten als Bachs
Helfer bei der Leipziger Kirchenmusik" (Bach-Jahrbuch 1984, pp. 45-52).
For the most detailed examination to date of the size and scope of the
"Bachische Collegium Musicum", see Don L. Smithers, "Bach, Reiche and the
Leipzig Collegia Musica", in Historic Brass Society Journal, ii, 1990,
pp. 1-51.

32. See Bach's "Eingabe an Kurfürst Friedrich August I. von
Sachsen" from December 31, 1725, fol. 5 verso, in BD I, p. 34 ff.

33. Public lecture, Christoph Wolff, "Bach's Collegium Musicum -
The Chamber Music Society of Leipzig," given at the Bruno Walter Audit-
orium, Lincoln Center, New York, September 12, 1984.

34. Wolff, New York lecture of 1984. For a number of specific details on the size and disposition of Bach's Leipzig Collegium Musicum,
see the references in note 31.

35. Besides the "Nahmens-Tag" music for King August III, performed
by the "Bachische Collegium Musicum... unter Trompeten und Paucken, im
Zimmermannischen Garten" on August 3, 1734, the other notable music for
the autumn of 1734 was BWV 215, performed by torch-light on October 5
outside the king's Leipzig residence, and the "CANTATA./.../ Thomana saß
annoch betrübt...(Anh. 19/ Neumann VIII) for the "Freudiger Willkomin..."
presented by the "Alumni der Thomana" on November 21, 1734 to greet the
"Hochedlen, Großachtbaren und Hochgelahrten" Magister Johann August
Ernesti, the "neuerwehlten" rector of St. Thomas and successor to Johann
Matthias Gesner (facs. of text books in Neumann 1974, p. 412 ff).

36. The specious theory of equating the number of surviving performing parts with the actual number of performers, as recently promulga-
ted by Joshua Rifkin and his admirers, is, of course, contradicted by a
variety of historical data, including Bach's own testimony and such
inferential evidence as, for example, the accounts of the Festmusik im
Collegium Musicum ("so unter Trompeten und Paucken Schall gehalten wurde")
performed over several days at Leipzig on the occasion of the coronation
celebrations for Churfürst Friedrich August II of Saxony as King August
III of Poland in the middle of January, 1734. Moreover, the disparity
between numbers of performers and performing parts associated with a
musical establishment like Dresden, for which there are reasonably accur-
ate accounts of singers and players as well as well-documented surviving
performance materials, underscores the dangers in attempting to equate
the one with the other. For a court like Munich at the time Orlandus
Lassus was the director of the Hoff-Musik, it is quite clear from what

Michael Praetorius says that the total number of ninety singers and players could never be verified by correlating performers with performance
materials.   Last, we should not be too hasty in judging the number of
performers who could read from one part. Sir John Hawkins, for example,
noted in his Musical History how in Italy "youths of fourteen or fifteen
play at sight over the shoulders of perhaps two or three persons standing
between them and the book."   Michel Corrette, too, noted in his violin
treatise that in his day several players were often obliged to read from
one part.

37. BD I, p. 60 ff.

38. "Since the year 17[?? - c. 1765] the usual double performances
of church music in St. Thomas and St. Nicolai on high feasts and other
holy days were discontinued. Until then there was music in both churches
on the first and second feast days of Easter, Pentecost, and Christmas,
and likewise on the other feast days. But upon the recommendation of the
Cantor Doles... it was resolved by the town council to discontinue the
music from the second choir." (Rost Nachricht, fol. 154)

39. Alfred Dürr, Die Kantaten von Johann Sebastian Bach. (Kassel:
1971), p. 65 ff.

40. Ibid., p. 66: "The consequences of this is that often an alarm-
ing number of copiest mistakes remain, which in no case during a performance (even if remembered from a rehearsal) could approximate the number
to be played correctly."

41. Ibid., p. 67: "No less revealing on this account is the
observation of what one does not find in the original parts to Bach´s
cantatas."

42. Concerning the alternation of performances by the erster Chor
in the two Hauptkirchen of Leipzig on the principal Sundays and/or holy
days during the year, see the comments of Christoph Ernst Sicul above (p.
166) and note 29.

43. The number of festivals for which there were double performances in the two Leipzig Hauptkirchen of St. Thomas and St. Nicolai is
not correctly given by Spitta.   In his biography of Bach (Fünftes Buch,
p. 15) he states that the lesser feasts requiring the erster Chor to sing
in both churches were "Neujahr-, Epiphanias-, Himmelfahrts- und Trinita-
tis-Tage, desgleichen am Tage Mariä Verkündigung...." The surviving text
books and other historical sources already cited make it clear that all
ten of the lesser feasts required a double performance by the erster Chor
in both churches.

44. See note 42.

PROGRAM OF CONFERENCE

Johann Sebastian Bach

INTERNATIONAL CONFERENCE

In Celebration: 1685 - 1750

Co-Sponsored by:
Lufthansa German Airlines

50*th* Anniversary 1935-1985

HOFSTRA
UNIVERSITY

HEMPSTEAD, NEW YORK 11550

THURSDAY, FRIDAY, SATURDAY
OCTOBER 24, 25, 26, 1985

HOFSTRA UNIVERSITY CULTURAL CENTER

Founding Director
JOSEPH G. ASTMAN
1916–1985

Interim Co-Directors
NATALIE DATLOF
ALEXEJ UGRINSKY

Special Assistant to the Director
BARBARA LEKATSAS

Development Coordinator
DONNA TESTA

Conference Coordinators
JO-ANN GRAZIANO MAHONEY
KARIN BARNABY

Secretaries
MARILYN SEIDMAN
ATHELENE A. COLLINS
PATRICIA A. CROSS

GALLERIES
David Filderman Gallery
MARGUERITE M. REGAN
Activities Coordinator

NANCY E. HERB
ANNE RUBINO
Gallery Staff

Emily Lowe Gallery
GAIL GELBURD
Director
MARY WAKEFORD
Executive Secretary

MUSICAL ORGANIZATIONS
American Chamber Ensemble
BLANCHE ABRAM
NAOMI DRUCKER
Directors

Hofstra String Quartet
SEYMOUR BENSTOCK
Artistic Director

President
JAMES M. SHUART

Conference Director
SEYMOUR L. BENSTOCK

Conference Coordinator
ATHELENE A. COLLINS

Conference Assistants

MUSA G. BADAT
KAREN CASTRO
MOHAMMED OMAR
IRA SILBERSTEIN
TARA STAHMAN

Conference Aides

REMELINE C. DAMASCO
PHILIP FRIED
WILLIAM KRUEGER
DIANE PATERSON

Johann Sebastian Bach Conference Committee

Carolyn Ackerman
William Hettrick

Natalie Datlof
Teri Noel Towe

Alexej Ugrinsky

DIRECTOR'S MESSAGE

The conference on Johann Sebastian Bach marks several important occasions for Hofstra University. First, is the fact of the great musician's tercentenary. Concomitantly, it is the University's 50th anniversary. Also, this is the first time since the conference events began here in 1976 that one has been devoted exclusively to a musical figure. This particular conference evokes for me a bitter-sweet feeling. The loss of our esteemed colleague, Dr. Joseph G. Astman, founder of the Hofstra University Cultural Center, which sponsors the conferences, has been a bitter blow. Never interfering and always supportive, his encouragement did much to bring the events of the conference together. The solid support of my colleagues at the Cultural Center, especially Natalie Datlof, Alexej Ugrinsky, Athelene A. Collins, Jo-Ann Graziano Mahoney, Marilyn Seidman and Patricia Cross cannot be overestimated. The enthusiastic efforts of our library staff must also be commended. All concerned realized the importance of this event celebrating the life of one of the greatest of musical giants.

Words really cannot express the genius of Johann Sebastian Bach. They are an attempt to verbalize his music and influence. There are few intellectual areas that have not been touched by his creativity. It has been my pleasure to sort out the many facets of these influences and assemble them for this occasion. The panels and concerts speak for themselves. My sincere thanks to all participants.

Seymour L. Benstock
Director
Johann Sebastian Bach Conference

Cover design -- The Logo

*The Logo for the Johann Sebastian Bach Tercentenary Conference is made up of two elements, his signature, many versions of which exist, and the monogram drawn from his signet ring. The monogram shows the letters J.S.B. and their interlocked reversal.

THURSDAY, OCTOBER 24, 1985

9:00 a.m. - 12:00 noon   **Registration**
                               Hofstra Hall Lobby, South Campus

---

CONFERENCE OPENING
10:00 a.m.   Hofstra University Cultural Center Lecture Hall
                               Hofstra University Library - First Floor

                               Greetings from the Hofstra University Community

                               James M. Shuart
                               President, Hofstra University

                               Seymour L. Benstock
                               Professor of Music
                               Conference Director

                               Greetings from the International Community

                               Christian Siebeck
                               Cultural Attaché
                               Consulate General of the Federal Republic of Germany
                               New York, NY

                               Peter Vincenz
                               First Secretary
                               Embassy of the German Democratic Republic
                               Washington, D.C.

                               Keynote Address: Gerhard Herz
                                                     Professor Emeritus of Music History
                                                     University of Louisville
                                                     Louisville, KY

                               "The Human Side of Bach Sources in America"

12:00 - 1:15 p.m.   **Lunch:** Student Center Cafeteria

12:00 - 5:30 p.m.   **Registration**
                               Dining Rooms ABC, Student Center, North Campus

---

1:30 p.m.   Dining Rooms ABC, Student Center, North Campus

                               Invitational Address: Harold E. Samuel
                                                          Yale University
                                                          New Haven, CT

                               "So You've Discovered a Bach Manuscript"

THURSDAY, OCTOBER 24, 1985 (Continued)

2:00 - 2:45 p.m.
FORUM I   **SOME CONTEMPORARY VIEWS OF BACH: THE CRITICS' VIEW**

                                             Moderator: Seymour L. Benstock
                                                      Department of Music
                                                      Hofstra University

Will Crutchfield
The New York Times

Peter Goodman
Newsday

Daniel Webster
The Philadelphia Inquirer

2:45 - 3:15 p.m.   **Invitational Address:** Martin Bookspan
                                                          Director of Artists & Repertoire
                                                          The Moss Music Group
                                                          New York, NY

"Symphony Orchestras and the Programming of Bach"

3:15 - 4:00 p.m.
FORUM II   **SOME CONTEMPORARY VIEWS OF BACH: THE COMPOSERS' VIEW**

                                             Moderator: Albert Tepper
                                                      Department of Music
                                                     Hofstra University

Elie Siegmeister
Professor Emeritus
Hofstra University

Lukas Foss
Composer & Conductor of
The Brooklyn Philharmonic & Milwaukee Symphony

James Primosch
Columbia University
New York, NY

4:00 - 5:30 p.m.   **PANEL Ia**
                                             Moderator: Jane S. Hettrick
                                                    Department of Fine Arts
                                                     Rider College
                                                     Lawrenceville, NJ

"Brandenburg Concerto No. 5: Bach as Innovator"
Doris P. Tishkoff
Oregon Institute of Technology
Klamath Falls, OR

THURSDAY, OCTOBER 24, 1985 (Continued)

PANEL Ia (continued)

"Tonal Integrity in Bach's Organ Works:
Its Attainment Through Organ Specification
and Registration"
Arthur Birkby
University of Wyoming
Laramie, WY

"Cyclical Perspectives in the Goldberg Variations"
Anne Wilson-Baxter
Miami University
Oxford, OH

4:00 - 5:30 p.m.

PANEL Ib
Moderator: Joann Krieg
            Department of English
            Hofstra University

"Fugue: Its Impact on Literature and Art"
Tim McCracken
Union County College
Cranford, NJ

"Bach and Edwards on the Religious Affections"
Richard A.S. Hall
Clarkson University
Potsdam. NY

"The Contemporizing of Scripture in the
Cantatas of Bach"
Howard C. Adams
Frostburg State College
Frostburg, MD

5:30 - 6:15 p.m.

Invitational Address: Teri Noel Towe
                            Ganz, Hollinger & Towe
                            New York, NY

"Early Recorded Performances of the Music of Bach:
Their Value to the Contemporary Performer and Scholar"

6:15 - 7:15 p.m.

Dinner: Student Center Cafeteria

7:15 - 8:15 p.m.

Emily Lowe Gallery, South Campus

Opening of Conference Exhibit

"The Life and Times of Johann Sebastian Bach"

Greetings: Hans E. Tausig
                President, Violin Society of America
                New York, NY

Invitational Address: Stephen R. Carpenter
                            North Bay, NY

"Toward a Visual Transcription of Bach's Compositions"

THURSDAY, OCTOBER 24, 1985 (Continued)

8:30 p.m.   Student Center Theater
                                              North Campus

GALA CONCERT

I SOLISTI DA CAMERA

Seymour L. Benstock, conductor

Raymond Erickson, harpsichord   Lionel Party, harpsichord

Samuel E. Baron, flute   Regis Iandiorio, violin

PROGRAM

Concerto in D minor BWV 1052
Allegro
Adagio
Allegro
Lionel Party, soloist

Suite in B minor BWV 1067
Ouverture
Rondeau
Sarabande
Bourees I and II
Polonaise and Double
Menuet
Badinerie
Samuel E. Baron, soloist

Interval

Concerto in C major BWV 1061
Allegro
Adagio ovvero Largo
Fuga
Lionel Party and Raymond Erickson, soloists

Brandenburg Concerto No. 5 in D major BWV 1050
Allegro
Affetuoso
Allegro
Regis Iandiorio, Samuel E. Baron and Raymond Erickson, soloists

Reception
(Sponsored by Schaller & Weber, Inc.)

ABOUT THE ARTISTS

SEYMOUR BENSTOCK, founder and conductor of I Solisti da Camera has had a long and distinguished career as conductor, cello soloist and chamber musician.   Currently Professor of Music at Hofstra University, he is the founder of the Hofstra Quartet, director of the University Orchestra and string programs.   He served in a similar capacity at Bowling Green University in Ohio and as assistant conductor of the Toledo Orchestra as well as a member of the BowArt Quartet and cellist of Columbia Artists "Music for Tonight" and principal cellist of the Hartford, Toledo and Naumburg orchestras.

I SOLISTI DA CAMERA, founded in 1978 is a highly select group of professional orchestral musicians each of whom is a soloist in his/her own right. They are known for their interpretation of the repertoire for chamber orchestra and have recently been heard in complete cycles of the Brandenburg Concerti and orchestral suites of Bach.

SAMUEL E. BARON, is one of the outstanding flutists and teachers of the present day. He has been affiliated with two distinguished chamber music groups, The New York Woodwind Quintet and the Bach Aria Group. He is presently teacher of flute at the Juillard School and Professor of Music at the State University of New York in Stony Brook.   In 1965 he was invited to become flute soloist of the famed Bach Aria Group and in 1980 assumed the musical directorship of the group.   Mr. Baron is organizer and director of the Bach Festival and Institute at Stony Brook.

RAYMOND ERICKSON, has played an important role in the study and performance of Baroque music in the United States.   He is director of the prestigious Aston Magna Academy which he founded in 1978.   Presently Professor of Music at the Aaron Copland School of Music at Queens College in New York, he was founding Director of the school where he now teaches harpsichord, music history and Baroque performance practice.   He has performed widely as soloist and recital partner with many distinguished Baroque figures, such as Jaap Schroeder, Michel Piget, Lionel Party and Sally Sanford.

REGIS IANDIORIO, first violinist of the Hofstra Quartet and an associate in music of the University is a graduate of the Manhattan and Juilliard Schools. He began his studies at the age of five with his father and later continued with such noted teachers as Louis Persinger, Sidney Harth, Oscar Shumsky and Raphael Bronstein. Formerly with the Pittsburgh Symphony, he has also served as concertmaster of the New York Pro Arte Chamber Orchestra and as a member of the New York Piano Trio.   Mr. Iandiorio has recorded for Paganiniana Records,The Musical Heritage Society and has been heard as soloist on New World Records.

LIONEL PARTY, a native of Chile, came to the United States as a Fulbright Scholar in 1970 to study with Albert Fuller at the Juilliard School. He is now a faculty member at the Juilliard, teaching harpsichord and Baroque music. Mr. Party has recorded for Desmar, Orion, Smithsonian and The Musical Heritage Society.   In addition to solo recitals in New York's major concert halls, he has appeared as soloist with the New York Philharmonic, Orpheus Chamber Orchestra, Solisti New York and the Waverly Consort.   Abroad he has appeared with the English Chamber Orchestra, South German Chamber Orchestra and the Collegium Instrumentale of Leipzig.   In 1972 he was awarded first prize in the J.S. Bach Fourth International Competition in Leipzig.

(Co-sponsored by the Music Performance Trust Fund of the American Federation of Musicians as arranged by Local 802)

FRIDAY, OCTOBER 25, 1985

9:00 a.m. - 5:30 p.m.   **Registration**
                               Dining Rooms ABC, Student Center, North Campus

9:00 - 10:30 a.m.   **PANEL IIa**
                               Moderator: Norman Walker
                                             Department of Performing Arts
                                             Adelphi University
                                             Garden City, NY

                               "Bach and the Dance"
                               Trudy Faber
                               Wittenburg University
                               Springfield, OH

                               Some Contemporary Dance Views of Bach
                               Discussants:
                               Susan F. Bindig
                               Mount Holyoke College
                               South Hadley, MA

                               Susan Matthews
                               Queens College/CUNY
                               New York, NY

9:00 - 10:30 a.m.   **PANEL IIb**
                               Moderator: Robert N. Keane
                                             Department of English
                                             Hofstra University

                               "The Message of J.S. Bach in Ingmar Bergman's
                               Cinematic Art"
                               Fritz Sammern-Frankenegg
                               University of Calfornia-Davis
                               Davis, CA

                               "J.S. Bach and Aldous Huxley"
                               Sister Ann Edward
                               Chestnut Hill College
                               Philadelphia, PA

                               "Bach's Musical Offering as Autobiography"
                               Steven A. Gottlieb
                               Quinnipiac College
                               Hamden, CT

10:30 a.m.   **Invitational Address:** Don O. Franklin
                                                          University of Pittsburgh
                                                          Pittsburgh, PA

                               "Problems of Tempo and Articulation in the Keyboard
                               Works of J. S. Bach: A New Look at the Sources"

FRIDAY, OCTOBER 25, 1985 (Continued)

11:00 a.m.   **Invitational Address:** Joshua Rifkin
                                                     Institute for Advanced Study
                                                     West Berlin
                                                     Federal Republic of Germany

                           "The Dispute over Bach's Chorus: The Case for Nonsense"

12:00 - 1:00 p.m.   **Lunch:** Student Center, North Campus

1:15 p.m.   **Invitational Address:** Paul Brainard
                                                     Princeton University
                                                     Princeton, NJ

                           "The Regulative and Generative Roles of Verse in Bach's
                           'Thematic' Invention"

2:00 - 3:30 p.m.   **PANEL IIIa**
                           Moderator: Laurence Libin
                                       Curator, Department of Musical Instruments
                                       The Metropolitan Museum of Art
                                       New York, NY

                           "Bach and the Flute"
                           Samuel Baron
                           SUNY/Stony Brook
                           Stony Brook, NY

                           Historical Instrument Making and Restoration:
                           Three Makers View Their Craft
                           Discussants:
                           George Bozeman, Jr. (Organs)
                           President, Bozeman Organs, Inc.
                           Deerfield, NH

                           Robert Meadows (Strings)
                           The Luthierie
                           Saugerties, NY

                           Robert Marvin (Woodwinds)
                           Eustis, ME

2:00 - 3:30 p.m.   **PANEL IIIb**
                           Moderator: Edgar Dittemore
                                       Department of Music
                                       Hofstra University

                           "Vocal Music: 'The St. John Passion'"
                           Eric Chafe
                           Brandeis University
                           Waltham, MA

                           "The Viola d'Amore in Bach's Time and Music"
                           Myron Rosenblum
                           Queensborough Community College/CUNY
                           New York, NY
                           (assisted by Amy Camus, viola da gamba;
                           David Pincus, tenor; Raymond Erickson, harpsichord)

FRIDAY, OCTOBER 25, 1985 (Continued)

PANEL IIIb (continued)

"Compositional Eclecticism in the Works of C.P.E. Bach, W.F. Bach, and Johann Müthel"
Pamela Fox
Miami University
Oxford, OH

3:30 p.m.

Invitational Address: Don Smithers
West Nyack, NY

"The Original Circumstances in the Performance of Bach's Leipzig Church Cantatas, 'Wegen seiner sonn- und festtägigen Amts-Verrichtungen'"

4:00 - 5:30 p.m.

PANEL IVa
Moderator: William E. Hettrick
Department of Music
Hofstra University

"Episodic Development and Motivic Expansion in the 'Die Kunst der Fuge' of Bach"
Adel Heinrich
Colby College
Waterville, ME

"Technical and Structural Aspects of the 'Two Part Inventions'"
Theodore O. Johnson
Michigan State University
East Lansing, MI

"The Calov Bible of Bach"
Ellis Finger
Lafayette College
Easton, PA

4:00 - 5:30 p.m.

PANEL IVb
Moderator: Richard Kramer
Department of Music
SUNY/Stony Brook
Stony Brook, NY

"Bach's Detractors"
H. Wendell Howard
St. John Fisher College
Rochester, NY

"Bach the Architect: Some Remarks on Structure and Pacing in Selected Praeludia"
Charles M. Joseph
Skidmore College
Saratoga Springs, NY

"Bach and the Trumpet"
Lydia Hailparn Ledeen
Drew University
Madison, NJ

FRIDAY, OCTOBER 25, 1985 (Continued)

EVENING PROGRAM

5:30 - 6:30 p.m.   David Filderman Gallery
                                    Hofstra University Library — Ninth Floor

                                    RECEPTION AND SPECIAL VIEWING

                                    "Eighteenth-Century Literary and Artistic Women"

6:30 - 8:30 p.m.   Dining Rooms ABC, North Campus

                                    JOHANN SEBASTIAN BACH CONFERENCE BANQUET

                                    Presiding: J. Richard Block
                                                     Assistant to the President
                                                     for Information Systems
                                                     Hofstra University

                                    Greetings: Robert C. Vogt
                                                     Dean, Hofstra College of Liberal Arts
                                                         and Sciences

8:30 p.m.   Student Center Theater, North Campus

CONCERT   **A Gala 22nd Anniversary Season**

                                    "A CLASSICAL VIEW OF THE FUGUE"

                                    THE HOFSTRA QUARTET

                                    Regis Iandiorio, violin
                                    Harry Zaratzian, viola
                                    Richard Henrickson, violin
                                    Seymour Benstock, cello

SATURDAY, OCTOBER 26, 1985

8:00 a.m. - 12:00 noon **Registration**
         Dining Rooms ABC, Student Center, North Campus

8:00 - 9:00 a.m.   Dining Rooms ABC, North Campus

          Continental Breakfast

9:00 - 11:00 a.m.   **PANEL V**
         Moderator: Howard Cinnamon
                Department of Music
                Hofstra University

         "The Unravelling of Schoenberg's Bach"
         John J. Daverio
         Boston University
         Boston, MA

         "Hemiola in the Eighteenth-Century"
         Vincent J. Corrigan
         Bowling Green State University
         Bowling Green, OH

         "Bach's 'Musical Offering': A Brief History,
         Analysis, and Interpretation"
         Miles V. Cowdrey
         Shippensburg University
         Shippensburg, PA

         "The Eclectic Bach: Stylistic Variety in the
         Introductory Movements to the Keyboard Suites"
         Donald C. Sanders
         Samford University
         Birmingham, AL

11:00 a.m. - 12:30 p.m. **PANEL VI**
         Moderator: Donald H. Crosby
                Department of Modern and Classical Language
                The University of Connecticut
                Storrs, CT

         "Bach the Orphan"
         Ernest D. May
         University of Massachusetts
         Amherst, MA

SATURDAY, OCTOBER 26, 1985 (Continued)

PANEL VI (continued)

"Bach Eclecticism as a Basis for Modern
Transcriptions and Arrangements"
Richard Pinnell
University of Wisconsin-La Crosse
La Crosse, WI

"Musical Expression and Musical Rhetoric
in the Harpsichord Works of J.S. Bach"
David Schulenberg
Stony Brook, NY

12:45 p.m.

Invitational Address: Douglas R. Hofstadter
University of Michigan
Ann Arbor, MI

"Writing Dialogues à la Bach"

A Complimentary Brunch will follow

Closing Remarks: Seymour Benstock

CREDIT for the success of the Johann Sebastian Bach Conference goes to more people than can be named herein, but those below deserve special commendation:

HOFSTRA UNIVERSITY OFFICERS
James M. Shuart, President
Emil V. Cianciulli, Chairman, Board of Trustees
Sanford Hammer, Provost and Dean of Faculties
J. Richard Block, Assistant to the President
    for Informational Systems
Anthony T. Procelli, Vice President
    for Finance and Treasurer
James Fellman, Vice President
    for Operational Services
Rochelle Lowenfeld, Vice President
    for Development
Robert C. Vogt, Dean, Hofstra College of
    Liberal Arts and Sciences

DEPARTMENT OF COMMUNICATION ARTS
William R. Renn, Chairman

DEPARTMENT OF MUSIC
Edgar Dittemore, Chairman

HOFSTRA UNIVERSITY LIBRARY
Charles R. Andrews, Dean
Wayne Bell, Assistant Dean

MAIL SERVICES
Dolores Pallingayan, Administrator
George McCue, Supervisor
Mail Room Staff

MEDIA SERVICES
Elizabeth Weston, Director
Ray Pynn, Assistant Director
Robert Cerro
William Gray

OPERATIONAL SERVICES
James Fellman, Vice President

Public Safety and Technical Services
Robert L. Crowley, Director
Edward N. Bracht, Deputy Director
  of Public Safety
Robert J. Kleinhans, Director
  of Technical Services

Facilities Management
Charles L. Churchill, Manager
Margaret A. Shields, Hospitality
  Services Manager
Dorothy Fetherston, Director
  of Scheduling
Anthony Internicola, Director
  of Dining Services
Dawn Smith, Assistant Director
  of Dining Services & Catering Manager

Theatre Facilities
Donald H. Swinney, Director
Jean Morris, Playhouse Manager

PUBLICATIONS OFFICE
Jack Ruegamer, Director,
  Printing & Publications
Vicki Anderson
Lisa San Sonette
Margaret Mirabella
Veronica Fitzwilliam
Doris Brown, Administrative Supervisor
  Printing Department
Printing Department Staff

SPECIAL SECRETARIAL SERVICES
Stella Sinicki, Supervisor
Secretarial Staff

UNIVERSITY RELATIONS
Harold A. Klein, Director
James Merritt, Assistant Director
M.F. Klerk, Editor/Writer
Frances B. Jacobsen, Administrative
  Assistant

COOPERATING INSTITUTIONS

American Federation of Musicians
New York, NY

Consulate General of the Federal Republic of Germany
New York, NY

Embassy of the German Democratic Republic
Washington, D.C.

German Information Center
New York, NY

Hewlett-Woodmere Public Library
Hewlett, NY

German Information Center
New York, NY

Inter Nationes
Federal Republic of Germany

Lufthansa German Airlines
East Meadow, NY

Nassau Library System
Uniondale, NY

Schaller & Weber, Inc.
Long Island City, NY

Suffolk County Library System
Bellport, NY

Special thanks to: Alex Shagin, Artist & Medalist
Los Angeles, CA

FORTHCOMING CONFERENCES:

November 7 - 8, 1985

"Sixteen Years of the United States Supreme Court
Under the Leadership of Chief Justice Warren E. Burger"

Director: Leon Friedman
            Hofstra University School of Law

November 14, 15, 16, 1985

"Avant-Garde Art and Literature: Toward a
Reappraisal of Modernism"

Honorary Chair of the Conference Committee: Françoise Gilot

Co-Directors: Pellegrino D'Acierno
                Department of Comparative Literature & Languages

                Barbara Lekatsas
                Hofstra University Cultural Center

November 19, 20, 21, 1985

"Television 1985-1986:   Issues for the Industry
and the Audience"

Director: J. Richard Block
            Assistant to the President for Informational Systems

December 10, 1985

"Maimonides: Philosopher/Educator"

Co-Directors: Henry Toledano
                Department of Comparative Literature and Languages

                Rabbi Moshe Sherman
                Department of Comparative Literature and Languages

Registration Programs available at the Conference Desk

🏛 HOFSTRA UNIVERSITY CULTURAL CENTER 🏛

Conference Schedule and Publications Listing

*George Sand Centennial—November 1976
*Heinrich von Kleist Bicentennial—November 1977
+ The Chinese Woman—December 1977
*George Sand: Her Life, Her Works, Her Influence—April 1978
*William Cullen Bryant and His America—October 1978
The Trotsky-Stalin Conflict in the 1920's—March 1979
Albert Einstein Centennial—November 1979
Renaissance Venice Symposium—March 1980
+ Sean O'Casey—March 1980
Walt Whitman—April 1980
Nineteenth-Century Women Writers—November 1980
Fedor Dostoevski—April 1981
Gotthold Ephraim Lessing—November 1981
Franklin Delano Roosevelt: The Man, the Myth, the Era—March 1982
Johann Wolfgang von Goethe—April 1982
James Joyce—October 1982
Twentieth-Century Women Writers—November 1982
Harry S. Truman: The Man from Independence—April 1983
**John Maynard Keynes—September 1983
Romanticism in the Old and the New World—Washington Irving, Stendhal, and Zhukovskii—October 1983
Espectador Universal: Jose Ortega y Gasset—November 1983
Dwight D. Eisenhower: Soldier, President, Statesman—March 1984
+ Victorian Studies—April 1984
Symposium on Eighteenth-Century Venice—April 1984
George Orwell—October 11-13, 1984
Friedrich von Schiller—November 8-10, 1984
John F. Kennedy: The Promise Revisited—March 28-30, 1985
Higher Education: Today and Tomorrow—April 18-19, 1985
Heritage: A Reappraisal of the Harlem Renaissance—May 2-4, 1985
Fourth Annual Edward F. Carlough Labor Law Conference—May 23-24, 1985
New York State History Conference—June 7-8, 1985
Eighteenth-Century Women and the Arts—October 10-12, 1985
Johann Sebastian Bach—October 24-26, 1985
Law School Conference: Sixteen Years of the Burger Court, 1969-1985—November 7-8, 1985
Avant-Garde Art and Literature—November 14-16, 1985
Television 1985-1986: Issues for the Industry and the Audience—November 19-21, 1985
Maimonides: Philosopher/Educator—December 10, 1985
Artificial Intelligence—February 27-March 1, 1986
Evolution of Business Education—March 13-14, 1986
Lyndon B. Johnson: A Texan in Washington—April 10-12, 1986
Fifth Annual Edward F. Carlough Labor Law Conference—April 1986
Long Island Studies—May 2-3, 1986
Attitudes Toward Persons with Disabilities—June 1986
The World of George Sand—October 16-18, 1986
Miguel Unamuno/Frederico Garcia-Lorca—November 1986
Carl Gustav Jung and the Humanities—November 24-26, 1986
Richard M. Nixon—Spring 1987
Bicentennial of the United States Constitution—October 1987
Aleksandr Sergeevich Pushkin—November 1987
Gerald R. Ford—Spring 1988
Byron and His Contemporaries—Spring 1988
Madame de Stael—October 1988
Jimmy Carter—Spring 1989
Bicentennial of the French Revolution—Fall 1989
Ronald Reagan—Spring 1990

*Volumes available from AMS Press, Inc.,
56 East 13th Street, New York, NY 10003

**Volume available from M.E. Sharpe, Inc.,
80 Business Park Drive, Armonk, NY 10504

+No publication
All other volumes forthcoming from Greenwood Press,
88 Post Road West, Westport, CT 06881

For further information and "Calls for Papers":
Hofstra University Cultural Center
Hofstra University
Hempstead, NY 11550
(516) 560-5669/5670

HOFSTRA
UNIVERSITY
HEMPSTEAD, NEW YORK 11550

"The Life and Times of
JOHANN SEBASTIAN BACH"

*An exhibit in celebration of the 300th anniversary
of the birth of Johann Sebastian Bach (1685-1750).*

EMILY LOWE GALLERY

HEMPSTEAD, NEW YORK 11550

THE LIFE AND TIMES OF JOHANN SEBASTIAN BACH

Director's Message

This exhibit is comprised of numerous items associated with Bach's life and times. They range from instruments and manuscripts of the period to more contemporary expressions inspired by the great master. Many areas in arts have been touched by Bach's genius and we see here assembled both original music manuscripts and some reproductions, also musical instruments either from his life time or recently made to recreate authentic sounds of the Baroque. A number of first editions and reproductions of significant literary materials dealing with Bach serve to enhance the conference and illuminate his genius. My thanks to the many contributors and the staff of the Emily Lowe Gallery.

Seymour L. Benstock
Conference Director
Johann Sebastian Bach Conference

Acknowledgements

Stephen Carpenter
North Bay, NY

Jack F. Pfeiffer
New York, NY

Concordia Seminary Library
St. Louis, MO

The Pierpont Morgan Library
New York, NY

Jacques Francais
New York, NY

Myron Rosenblum
Sunnyside, NY

Robert Meadow
Saugerties, NY

Albert Tepper
Levittown, NY

Teri Noel Towe
New York, NY

Exhibit   151

JOHANN SEBASTIAN BACH
(1685–1750)

EXHIBITION CATALOGUE

1. Lithograph, Handel, Bach and Scalatti
    In celebration of the tercentenary of their births
    This edition is limited to 300 copies, each hand signed and numbered
    by the artist

    Donated by Alex Shagin, Artist and Medalist
    Los Angeles, CA

2. Baroque violin (anonymous)
    Converted by Thomas Williams, student of Robert Meadow

    Contributed by Robert Meadow, Saugerties, NY

3. Cello, (circa 18th century, anonymous)
    Restored and converted to Baroque disposition by Robert Meadow.

    Contributed by Robert Meadow, Saugerties, NY

4. Modern violin by Robert Meadow
    Displayed for comparative purposes.

    Contributed by Robert Meadow, Saugerties, NY

5. Score of Bach's B minor Mass with signatures of members of the
    Dresseldorf Bach Society, dated 1872.

    Contributed by Albert Tepper, Levittown, NY

6. 12 Wall pieces by Stephen Carpenter, based on the themes
    of Bach's "Kunst der Fuge".

    6.1   Contrapunctus 1 – Simple Fugue
    6.2   Contrapunctus 2 – Simple Fugue
    6.3   Contrapunctus 4 – Simple Fugue
    6.4   Contrapunctus 5 – Stretto
    6.5   Contrapunctus 7 – Augmentation
    6.6   Contrapunctus 8 – Triple
    6.7   Contrapunctus 9 – Double
    6.8   Contrapunctus 10 – Double
    6.9   Contrapunctus 12 – Canon
    6.10 Contrapunctus 15 – Canon in contrary motion and augmentation
    6.11 Contrapunctus 16 – Mirror Fugue
    6.12 Contrapunctus 18 – Quadruple Fugue

    Contributed by Stephen Carpenter, North Bay, NY

7. Cantata no. 112. Der Herr ist mein getreuer Hirt
    (The Lord is my faithful shepherd.)
    Autograph manuscript of the full score
    Shown are the first and last page

    This is one of three cantatas Bach wrote for the Second Sunday after
    Easter (Misericordias Domini). It was first performed in Leipzig on
    8 April 1731. The text is the version of the 23rd Psalm by Wolfgang
    Musculus. Both the Epistle and the Gospel for the day has to do with
    sheep going astray and with the good Shepherd.

    Mary Flagler Cary Music Collection
    Contributed by The Pierpoint Morgan Library, New York, NY

8. Autograph letter signed, dated Leipzig, November 2, 1748, to his
    cousin Johann Elias Bach in Schweinfurt

    This is the last known letter in Bach's hand. In it he writes of
    family affairs, and thanks his cousin for a cask of wine. But the
    cask arrived nearly two-thirds empty, and Bach had to pay so many
    carriage, coustoms, and delivery charges that each quart cost him
    nearly five Groschen —"which for a gift is really too expensive."

    Mary Flagler Cary Music Collection.
    Contributed by The Pierpont Morgan Library, New York, NY

9. Cantata no. 171. Gott, wie dein Name, so ist auch dein Ruhm
    (God, as Thy name, so is Thy glory.) Autograph manuscript of the
    full score. Pages shown are 1 and 5.

    This cantata, for the Feast of the Circumcision, was composed in 1729
    or a few years later. Bach frequently used music from on composition
    in another: in Cantate 171 the opening chorus omnipotentem" from this
    B-minor Mass; the final chorale is identical to one found in another
    church cantata; and the music from the aria "Jesus shall be my first
    word in the New Year" had earlier been used in a secular cantata in
    an aria praising the gentle west wind.

    On deposit in the Morgan Library; lent by Robert Owen Lehman.
    Contributed by The Pierpont Morgan Library, New York, NY

10. The Bach/Calov Bible
    Reverend Louis Brighton, photographer
    Photographs of the family bible of Johann Sebastian Bach with
    notations in his own handwriting.

    Contributed by the Concordia Seminary Library, St. Louis, MO

11. Autograph of receipt of monies from the "Lobwsser Legacy,"
    dated 1750 and signed by Hulse, Bach and Krigel
    Authenticatd by Charles Hamilton and willed to Mr. Jack F. Pfeiffer
    by Wanda Landowska

    Contributed by Jack F. Pfeiffer, New York NY

Exhibit   153

12. Guitar, by Joachim Tielke of Germany (1641-1719), dated 1679
     Contributed by Jacques Francais, Rare Violins, Inc., New York, NY

13. Violin, by Hendrick Jacobs (1630-1699), labelled Amati, (circa 1700)
     Contributed by Jacques Francais, Rare Violins, Inc., New York, NY

14. Violin, by Jacobus Stainer (1621-1683), of Austria, dated 1675
     Contributed by Jacques Francais, Rare Violins, Inc., New York, NY

15. Violin, by Antonio (circa 1540 - n.d.) and Hieronymous
     Amati (1561-1630), of Italy. The instrument is dated 1629
     Contributed by Jacques Francais, Rare Violins, Inc., New York, NY

16. Pochette, (Kit) by Nicolo Gagliano (1675-1763), of Italy
     with original neck
     Contributed by Jacques Francais, Rare Violins, Inc., New York, NY

17. Baroque French Violin, (mid 18th century) with original neck and
     bass bar
     Contributed by Jacques Francais, Rare Violins Inc., New York, NY

18. Gamba bow, circa 1740
     Contributed by Jacques Francais, Rare Violins Inc., New York, NY

19. Transitional bow, circa 1780
     Contributed by Jacques Francais, Rare Violins Inc., New York, NY

20. Piccolo Violin, by Joseph (1726-1793) and Antonio Gagliano
     (1728-1805) of Italy, dated 1795 with original neck and bass bar
     Contributed by Jacques Francais, Rare Violins Inc., New York, NY

21.   Viola d'amore by Johannes Udalricus Eberle (1699-1768) of
     Czechoslovia, dated Progue 1732.

     Contributed by Myron Rosenblum, Sunnyside, NY

22. <u>Programme Book for the Second Bach Festival held by the Neue Bach
     Gesellchaft, in Leipzig, October 1-3, 1904</u>

     The programme book is opened to the pages listing the Directors and
     Musical Advisors of the Neue Bach Gesellschaft. Among the directors
     is the violinist Joseph Joachim, and among the Musical Advisors are
     the concert pianists Ferruccio Bosoni and Eugen d'Albert, the
     composer Gustav Mahler, and the conductor Felix von Weingartner.

     Contributed by Teri Noel Towe, New York, NY

23. <u>Programme Book for the Third Bach Festival held by the Neue Bach
     Gesellschaft, in Eisenach, May 26-28, 1907</u>

     The Third Bach Gestival was held in conjunction with the dedicatiobn
     of the Bach-Museum, which is located in what was then erroneously
     considered to be the house in which Bach was born. The book is
     opened to the frontispiece of the section pertaining to the
     dedication of the Museum.

     Contributed by Teri Noel Towe, New York, NY

24. <u>Programme for the Fifth Bach Festival</u> held by the Neue Bach <u>Gesellschaft, in Duisburg, June 4-7, 1910</u>

The book is opened to the program of a concert featuring the harpsichordist Wanda Landowska. Her appearances at the Festival in 1910, however, were not the first by a harpsichordist at the Neue Bach Gesellschaft Festivals. Max Seiffert, for example, played harpsichord continuo at the Festivals in 1904 and 1907

Contributed by Teri Noel Towe, New York, NY

25. <u>Programme Books (2) for the Twenty-Second Bach Festival</u> held by the <u>Neue Bach Gesellschaft, in Leipzig, June 21-24, 1935</u>

One of the books is opened to the pages containing the programmes for a series of recitals given on historic organs in the vicinity of Leipzig, including the organ in the Dorfkirche in Stormthal, built by Zacharias Hildebrandt and dedicated by Bach on November 2, 1723.

Contributed by Teri Noel Towe, New York, NY

26. <u>Programme Books (2) for the Twenty-Seventh Bach Festivals, 1950</u>

Because of the division of Germany into Eastern and Western Zones, two Bach Festivals were held concurrently in Germany in 1950 to commemorate the 200th anniversary of the death of Sebastian Bach. The Festival in the West was held in Göttingen; the Festival in the East was held in Leipzig. Only the Leipzig Festival was held under the auspices of the Neue Bach Gesellschaft, which is based in Leipzig, although a gathering of NBG members was held at the Göttingen Festival.

Contributed by Teri Noel Towe, New York, NY

27. <u>The first volume of the Bach Gesellschaft Edition of the complete</u> <u>works of Johann Sebastian Bach, containing the Cantatas, BWV 1 - 10,</u> <u>published in 1851</u>

Previously in the collection of the pioneer British early music specialist Arnold Goldsbrough, this volume is a "plate" copy specially bound for a subscriber to the Bach Gesellschaft Edition. The volume is open to the frontispiece, perhaps the most universally known engraving based on the 1746 Haussmann portrait of Sebastian Bach.

Contributed by Teri Noel Towe, New York, NY

Exhibit   155

28.   The sixth volume of the Bach Gesellschaft Edition of the complete
      works of Johann Sebastian Bach, containing the Mass in B Minor, BWV
      232, published in 1856

      From the same set as the first volume, this plate copy of Volume 6 of
      the Bach Gesellschaft Edition contains two versions of the "Credo",
      "Sanctus", "Osanna", and "Dona Bobis Pacem" of the Mass.   This
      anomaly, explained in detail in Gerhard Herz's The Performance
      History of Bach's B Minor Mass, was the result of the refusal by the
      then owner of the autograph score, Hermann Nageli, to make it
      available to the Editors of the bach Gesellschaft.   Initially, the
      "Kyrie" and "Gloria" were printed from the parts that Bach sent to
      the Electoral Court in Dresden in 1733; the "Sanctus" was printed
      from the parts Bach had prepared in 1724; and the balance of the Mass
      from a copy of the full score made under the aegis of Carl Philipp
      Emanuel Bach.   Within a few weeks after the publication of the sixth
      Volume, the Editors of the Bach Gesellschaft obtained the autograph
      score and provided subscribers to the Edition with a replacement for
      all but the "Kyrie" and "Gloria" of the Mass and advised them to
      discard the "original" edition of the "Credo", "Santus", "Osanna",
      and "Dona Nobis Pacem" that they had been sent.   A few subscribers
      disregarded these instructions and had both versions bound together,
      seriatim.   These copies are great rarities.   This particular example
      has been opened to the beginning of the "Et expecto" in the version
      of the "Credo" subsequently replaced by the edition based on the
      autograph.

      In light of this curious history, it is something of an irony, then,
      that the copy that was used as the basis for the first version of the
      "Credo", "Osanna", and "Dona Nobis Pacem" is a more accurate edition
      of these segments of the Mass than the one based on the autograph,
      because the Editors, of the Bach Gesellschaft were unaware that Carl
      Philipp Emanuel Bach had apprently "touched up" his father's
      autograph as a guide to the copyist who prepared the parts for a
      performance of the "Credo" of the Mass that C. P. E. Bach gave in
      Hamburg in 1786.

      Contributed by Teri Noel Towe, New York, NY

29.   John Nikolaus Forkel: Über Johann Sebastian Bachs Leben, Kunst und
      Kunstwerke, published in 1802

      Published by Hoffmeister & Kühnel in Leipzig in 1802, this invaluable
      book is the first monograph on the life and works of Johann Sebastian
      Bach.   For it Forkel obtained most of his information from Bach's
      elder sons Wilhelm Friedemann and Carl Philipp Emanuel.   Like most of
      the known copies of the first edition, this example is missing its
      frontispiece, which has been razored out becaused, to use modern
      parlance, it was "suitable for framing".   A photographic reproduction
      of the frontispiece has been laid in to this copy.

      Contributed by Teri Noel Towe, New York, NY

30. __Johann Sebastian Bach: Figured, Transposed Organ Continuo Part to__
     __the Cantata, Christ unser Herr zum Jordan Kam, BWV 7__

Principally in the hand of Christian Gottlieb Meissner, Bach's chief
copyist during his first years as Director musices in Leipzig, this
organ player's part is the only part from any of the 44 such sets of
parts that Bach's widow, Anna Magdalena, gave to the Leipzig city
Council (in exchange for a half year's worth of her husband's
slavery) that is no longer in Leipzig. Since the whereabouts of the
composing score for the Cantata are not known, this part and the
others in the set, which are now in the Bach-Archiv in Leipzig, are
the primary score for the work.   The third cantata in the second
jahrgang composed at Leipzig, _Christ unser Herr zum Jordan kam_ was
written for performance on the Feast of St. John the Baptist, and was
heard for the first time on June 24, 1724.

Since a very early stage in its history, the part has been missing
its second sheet - pages 3 and 4 - which contain the last third of
the opening chorus and all of the aria for bass and coninuo "Merkt
und hört, ihr Menschenkinder". (A less than scrupulous bass probably
absconded with the paage rather than copy the elaborate continuo out
for himself.)   Late in the summer of 1808, the part was given by
August Eberhard Muller (1767-1817), the Cantor of the _Thomosschule,_
to Haydn's student, the composer Sigismund Neukomm (1778-1858), when
he passed through Leipzig on his way to Vienna from St. Petersburgh,
Russia. Neukomm recorded this event, but not, alas, the exact date,
on the top of the first page of tghe manuscript. After his death,
the part disappeared until 1913, when it was sold by ther Berlin rare
book and autograph dealer Leo Liepmanssohn. It disappeared again,
until 1934, when it was bought by a gentleman from New England who
gave it to his son as a 21st birthday present. In 1983, it was sold
again, at auction by Phillips Son & Neale, Inc., in New York; at that
time it was acquired by its present owner.

Although the notes themselves, as well as most of the headings, were
copied out by Meissner, the continuo figures, the dynamic markings,
and perhaps a couple of the movement headings were written in by
Bach.

The part, which was bound in red morocco in England in the mid-19th
century, has been opened to the 2nd and 5th pages.

Contributed by Teri Noel Towe, New York, NY

Index

About the Editor
and Contributors

THE EDITOR

SEYMOUR L. BENSTOCK is Professor of Music at Hofstra where, in addition to his academic duties in the areas of music history and literature and head of the string department, he is the conductor of the Hofstra Symphony Orchestra, cellist, founder and artistic director of the Hofstra Quartet and has served as Director of the Music Program of the Hofstra Cultural Center. Also, he has authored A Workbook in the Elements of Music, contributed articles to The New Grolier International Encyclopedia and recently completed a monograph "Venice: Four Centuries of Instrument Making" (Journal of the Violin Society of America). Professor Benstock holds degrees in performance and musicology and has also been Music Editor of the Sentinel-Tribune (Ohio).

HOWARD C. ADAMS is Professor of English at Frostburg State University in Maryland. He holds the Ph.D. degree in English from Pennsylvania State University and has also studied at Northwestern, Columbia, Rutgers and Colgate Rochester Divinity School. Professor Adams has served churches as Director of Christian Education and Music for two years and as pastor for twelve years. His publications include articles on Benjamin Colman, a colonial poet and clergyman, John Ford and William Shakespeare.

SAMUEL BARON is the Music Director of the world renowned Bach Aria Group. In addition, he is flutist of the New York Woodwind Quintet and Professor of Music at the State University of New York at Stony Brook. Among his many recordings are two complete performances of the Bach sonatas for flute and harpsichord and flute and continuo, the first dating from 1970 (Musical Heritage) and the more recent one from 1991 (Soundspells).

SISTER ANN EDWARD BENNIS of the Sisters of Saint Joseph has served as Professor of English at Chestnut Hill College in Philadelphia. Her graduate work was done at Catholic University of America and the University of Pennsylvania. In addition, she has studied at Oxford University and

the University of London. Her areas of specialization include philology
and Chaucer.   Sister Bennis has translated from the French, The Martyrs
of Privas, an account from the early history of her community in France.
She served on the editorial staff on the British annual publication Bibliography of Language and Literature.

VINCENT CORRIGAN has degrees in music education, piano, harpsichord and
holds a Ph.D. in Musicology from Indiana University. His primary
research interests lie in the music of the troubadours and trouvères as
well as the polyphony of the 12th and 13th centuries, and Baroque performance practice. He is currently Associate Professor of Music at Bowling
Green State University in Ohio.   His publications include articles in
International Music Journals and transcriptions in The Medieval Lyric.

JOHN J. DAVERIO holds the Ph.D. in Musicology from Boston University
where he is currently Associate Professor of Music, Chairman of the
Musicology Department and Director of the Graduate School Division of
Music.   He has published a variety of articles on 17th-and 19th-century
topics in Acta Musicologica, The Journal of Musicological Research
and The Journal of Musicology. He received the Alfred Einstein Award
from the American Musicological Society in 1988 for his work on Robert
Schumann and is now completing a monograph on the ties between German
Romantic music and literature.

FRITZ SAMMERN-FRANKENEGG was born and educated in Austria where he
received the Ph.D. from the University of Vienna. He was a lecturer at
the University of Gothenburg, Sweden and currently teaches German and
Swedish language, literature and film at the University of California
(Davis). He is the author of two television series on Ingmar Bergman's
art of film: Ingmar Bergman's Secret Message in "The Silence"
(1985) and The Message of Johann Sebastian Bach in Ingmar Bergman's
Cinematic Art (1989).

STEVEN A. GOTTLIEB is Professor and Chair of English at Quinnipiac
College in Connecticut. He is a senior editor of Issues in Integrative
Studies, and his ongoing work includes several studies of Richard Wagner
and of Darwin and Natural Theology. In addition, he has written articles
on "Bach's B Minor Mass as Drama," and Wagnerian opera production. His
"The Case Against Wilhelm Furtwängler's Conducting" will appear in The
Journal of the Wilhelm Furtwängler Society of America.

RICHARD A. SPURGEON HALL holds the B.A. from Boston University, the M.A.
from Dalhousie University and the Ph.D. from the University of Toronto,
all three degrees being in the discipline of philosophy. His specialties
are in the history of American philosophy, the philosophy of religion and
the philosophy of art. He has published The Neglected Northampton
Texts of Jonathan Edwards.   Professor Hall currently teaches at the
Center for Liberal Studies at Clarkson University and holds a research
appointment at the State University of New York at Potsdam. In addition,
he serves as managing editor of The Edwardean: Studies in the Thought
of Jonathan Edwards and as director of the Edwards Series for the Edwin
Mellen Press.

CHARLES M. JOSEPH is Professor of Music at Skidmore College. He holds the Ph.D. from the University of Cincinnati and has done post-doctoral work at Harvard and Yale. As a result of study with Cristoff Wolf, he published an article, "Some Revisional Aspects of Bach's Keyboard Partitas, BWV 827 and 830" for the Riemenschneider Bach Institute. He is the author of the book Stravinsky and the Piano as well as numerous articles which have appeared in such publications as The Musical Quarterly, The Journal of Musicology, The Journal of Music Theory, Music Theory Spectrum, and the New Grove Dictionary of American Music.

DAVID SCHULENBERG holds the Ph.D. from the State University of New York at Stony Brook. He has taught at Columbia University, the University of Texas and the University of Delaware. His publications include The Keyboard Music of J. S. Bach and The Instrumental Music of C.P.E. Bach. Professor Schulenberg's contribution to the present volume is based on research undertaken while holding an Andrew Mellon fellowship at New York University (1984-1985).

DON L. SMITHERS holds the Ph.D. in the History of Music from Oxford University. As a noted trumpet performer, he has appeared with the Robert Shaw Chorale, the New York Cantata Singers and as a cornetto player with the New York Pro Musica. While in England he became a founding member of Musica Reservata, The Early Music Consort and The London Cornetto and Sackbut Ensemble. For several years, he was Associate Professor of Music History at Syracuse University and also was appointed Docent for the History of Musical Performance and Director of the Collegium Musicum at the Royal Dutch Conservatory of Music in The Hague. He is a contributor to the New Grove Dictionary of Music and Musicians, has recently published articles in the Bach-Jahrbuch, and is presently at work on a monumental four-volume study on the music, history, manufacture and use of the trumpet from classical antiquity until the era of Beethoven. Professor Smithers is also the author of The Music and History of the Baroque Trumpet before 1721.

Hofstra University's
Cultural and Intercultural Studies
Coordinating Editor, Alexej Ugrinsky

Faith of a (Woman) Writer
(Editors: Alice Kessler-Harris and William McBrien)

José Ortega y Gasset: Proceedings of the *Espectador universal* International
Interdisciplinary Conference
(Editor: Nora de Marval-McNair)

George Orwell
(Editors: Courtney T. Wemyss and Alexej Ugrinsky)

John F. Kennedy: The Promise Revisited
(Editors: Paul Harper and Joann P. Krieg)

Lyndon Baines Johnson and the Uses of Power
(Editors: Bernard J. Firestone and Robert C. Vogt)

Eighteenth-Century Women and the Arts
(Editors: Frederick M. Keener and Susan E. Lorsch)

Suburbia Re-examined
(Editor: Barbara M. Kelly)

James Joyce and His Contemporaries
(Editors: Diana A. Ben-Merre and Maureen Murphy)

The World of George Sand
(Editors: Natalie Datlof, Jeanne Fuchs, and David A. Powell)

Richard M. Nixon: Politician, President, Administrator
(Editors: Leon Friedman and William F. Levantrosser)

Watergate and Afterward: The Legacy of Richard M. Nixon
(Editors: Leon Friedman and William F. Levantrosser)

Immigration and Ethnicity: American Society—"Melting Pot" or
"Salad Bowl"?
(Editors: Michael D'Innocenzo and Josef P. Sirefman)